YORK NOTES

General Editors: Professor A.N. Jeffares (*University of Stirling*) & Professor Suheil Bushrui (*American University of Beirut*)

Charlotte Brontë

JANE EYRE

Notes by Barty Knight

OBE MA (CAMBRIDGE)

LONGMAN
YORK PRESS

YORK PRESS
Immeuble Esseily, Place Riad Solh, Beirut.

LONGMAN GROUP UK LIMITED
Longman House, Burnt Mill, Harlow,
Essex CM20 2JE, England
and Associated Companies throughout the world

First published 1980
Fourth impression 1987

ISBN 0-582-78098-5

Produced by Longman Group (FE) Ltd
Printed in Hong Kong

Contents

Part 1

Introduction

The life of Charlotte Brontë

Charlotte Brontë was born in 1816, the third of six children, five girls and a boy. Their father, Patrick Brontë, was a clergyman who came from Ireland. Their mother came from an intelligent family in Cornwall, in the extreme south-west of England. Although the Brontë children were thus a mixture of Irish and Cornish stock they had no experience of either Ireland or Cornwall. They were born in Yorkshire, lived most of their lives in that northern part of England, and felt themselves to belong there.

Their mother died soon after the sixth child was born and soon after the family had moved to a place called Haworth, a large village in a wild area of hilly moorland in the West Riding of Yorkshire. The family home was the parsonage, the residence assigned to Mr Brontë as local clergyman. It was a solid, well-built house, but not more than moderately comfortable. When the father was left a widower with six children he arranged for his dead wife's sister to act as housekeeper. Although she seems to have been a respectable and dutiful person she never ceased to regret being obliged to spend her life in windswept Yorkshire instead of in sunny Cornwall. Thus she never became a warm or loving substitute for the mother the six children had lost.

Before Charlotte reached the age of ten her two elder sisters both died, leaving her the eldest of the remaining four children. The brother, Branwell, was next in age to her. Then came Emily and finally Anne. The father, although a talented man, became increasingly odd in his behaviour and theories. The son, also very talented, proved a disappointing failure and finally a disgrace. Neither contributed anything beneficial or useful to the exertions of Charlotte and her two sisters.

The events of their lives may be simply stated. In 1824 the two eldest sisters were sent off to a boarding school for 'the daughters of clergymen', called Cowan Bridge School in the north-west of Yorkshire. They both died of tuberculosis, probably because the school was not a good one. Charlotte and Emily were also sent to Cowan Bridge for short periods while still absurdly young, about eight and six respectively. The deaths of the older sisters probably saved them from a similar fate, and they were mercifully removed. Charlotte, however, was old enough to retain a vivid recollection of the sufferings and miseries that marked the daily routine of the girls boarding at Cowan Bridge. They were probably the first formative stimulus in her development as a creative writer, just as Lowood in the book is seen to be a strongly formative influence in the early development of Jane's character. There is an unquestionably autobiographical quality in the writing of the first part of *Jane Eyre.*

For several more years the four surviving children then lived at home and were left almost entirely to themselves. It must be recalled that they were still astonishingly young. Even Charlotte, the eldest, had yet to reach the age of ten when this period started. They received a little formal teaching from their father and aunt, but for the most part studied and learnt, read and played, more or less as their spirits moved them. If they had been commonplace, merely average children, they would probably have learnt very little. They might even have remained barely literate, as did many labourers' and farmers' daughters when similarly neglected. But the spirits that moved the Brontë children were intensely alive and vigorous. The almost complete lack of any formal education proved in many ways to be a positive benefit. Their imaginations were encouraged to be active. They read at their own speeds. They wrote what they wanted to write. They had a strong community or team spirit, with a great deal of lively conversation and discussion, and a profitable cross-fertilisation of ideas and opinions. There was a strong bond of sympathy among them. When Branwell, later in life, proved to be a failure, the three sisters suffered greatly; but their own interdependence, love and loyalty endured until, one by one, they died. During the time of their 'home education' they all became 'writers'. Naturally enough they did not receive any payment for what they wrote. Nothing was offered for sale; nothing was sold. But their attitudes to writing were already professional. They wrote stories and plays because they wanted to write them, not because they were told to write them. They corrected, revised and improved them, not because a teacher required it but because they were already in search of artistic rightness and perfection. As creative writers they were virtually adult and mature at an age when many children can hardly be persuaded to complete a school exercise conscientiously.

The sisters did receive a few more odd fragments of organised teaching. Charlotte herself, at the age of fifteen, went to Roe Head, a much better school than Cowan Bridge. She stayed there for a year and a half, and made at least two good friends. Then followed another period at home when she was largely responsible for educating Emily and Anne (out of what she herself had learnt at Roe Head). When she was nineteen, Charlotte spent some time at Roe Head as a junior assistant teacher. For part of this time Emily was also there as a pupil, to be later replaced by Anne. Neither Emily nor Anne was happy at Roe Head, and soon all three sisters were back once more at Haworth.

Charlotte and Anne both had some experience as governesses, or privately employed teachers. The lives of governesses varied greatly. In some households they lived pleasant lives, but in others conditions were probably unpleasant, since governesses were often expected to work in virtually impossible circumstances. They were supposed to teach the family's children effectively and to impose discipline, yet the pupils were permitted to treat them as social inferiors.

Neither Charlotte nor Anne was lucky enough to find one of the better posts; and neither stayed in her job for long. Charlotte decided that it would be more satisfactory for them to open a school of their own. She and Emily, both now in their twenties, spent some time at a school in Brussels, in order to improve their teaching qualifications. Later Charlotte returned to the Brussels school as a junior teacher, but experienced the great unhappiness of falling in love with Monsieur Heger, the husband of the Madame Heger for whom she was working. She returned to Haworth, and the three sisters made renewed efforts to launch the school they had planned. Family circumstances prevented this, and the undistinguished teaching careers of the three sisters were over.

Nevertheless their experiences provided much of the material of the novels to which they then turned. In *Jane Eyre* itself, quite apart from the long phase of Jane's girlhood placed inside the disgraceful institution of Lowood, Jane's further employment at Thornfield is as a governess. There are frequent unkind and offensive comments made on governesses in general by Blanche Ingram and the other ladies visiting Thornfield; both Diana and Mary Rivers are employed as governesses in, we are led to suppose, not very pleasant households; and when Jane gets herself a new post in Morton it is as village schoolmistress. Charlotte Brontë's attitude to the employment of women in education, whether public or private, reflects pretty accurately the three sisters' real-life experiences in schools and private homes.

When Charlotte herself was approaching the age of thirty, and Emily and Anne not much younger, they settled down once more to their life of writing, this time determining to become genuine professionals if possible. In 1847 Emily's one and only novel, *Wuthering Heights,* and Anne's slighter work, based on the life of a governess, *Agnes Grey,* were both accepted for publication while Charlotte's first novel, *The Professor,* was still being rejected. It was then, refusing to be downhearted, that Charlotte embarked on *Jane Eyre.* This was immediately popular, becoming and remaining one of the most successful of all English novels.

In the two years that followed Branwell, Emily and Anne all died. At the age of thirty-two, with no more than the memory of a hopeless love for a married man beyond her reach, Charlotte found herself the last survivor of a family of six children. She had, in particular, lost Emily and Anne with whom all her previous writings had been critically and warmly discussed. With characteristic resolution she continued to write – although never as successfully again – and cultivated a wider circle of friends. Eventually she married one of her father's curates, but experienced not more than a few months of happiness with him before dying herself in 1855, a little before her thirty-ninth birthday.

Historical background

Born in the year after Waterloo, Charlotte Brontë grew up in an England that was moving steadily in the direction of becoming Europe's most stable and prosperous country. The industrial revolution was proceeding apace; the railway age would soon begin; steam engines were already being used in mines, factories and ships; small towns were beginning to swell into smoky centres of manufacturing industry; and all this was taking place under a government and legislature that were still narrowly restricted to the privileged few, who were wealthy by birth or becoming wealthy in commerce.

Despite the industrial revolution, the factories, mills, mines and workshops, England was still an almost entirely agricultural country. The population was small. Even those who lived in the town were within easy reach of the country, and the country was largely beautiful. The rich lived in elegant homes, the middle class in comfortable homes, and even the poor for the most part lived in pleasant, if primitive, cottages. The English countryside was a part of everyone's existence.

The industrial revolution, however, was just beginning to bring dirt and squalor, ugliness and crime, into the lives of the poor whom circumstances forced to live and work in the mills and factories of the new towns. By the time Charlotte Brontë was writing *Jane Eyre* there was a growing realisation of the price that was being paid for this new prosperity. Labourers were being unfairly treated without redress, women workers were also ill-treated and underpaid, both in their homes and in the mills, while children were often overworked in abominable conditions.

Little of this is seen in *Jane Eyre*. Apart from passing references to a few towns and the nation's capital city the entire action of *Jane Eyre* is not only passed in the country but is unaffected by affairs elsewhere, political or commercial.

Society in the country was still effectively feudal. A small agricultural community was still more or less governed by the landlord or 'lord of the manor' to whom rents were paid by tenants of farms or cottages. Such a landlord was usually a magistrate into the bargain. Mrs Reed is the widow of one such landowner; Mr Rochester is another and Mr Oliver a third. No one else in the rural community had much authority except for the local parson, like St John Rivers, or to a lesser extent an apothecary or surgeon, such as Mr Lloyd or Mr Carter. The social structure was largely well-ordered and accepted. On the whole it was reasonably fair and humane. Such was the society in which Charlotte Brontë grew up and such is the setting she provides for her heroine.

Literary background

By the time Charlotte Brontë was born England was ready for the rapid growth of the novel. Many more people could read than ever before; the theatres were 'disreputable', possibly even 'immoral'; poetry, especially Byron's, was popular but was not a very good medium for telling a story. And that is what thousands of men and women wanted – more and more large-scale stories, novels spread preferably over three volumes. In the first half of the nineteenth century the English became a nation of avid novel-readers.

As soon as they too could read, Charlotte Brontë and her sisters could comprehend this situation. There was something even more important. No woman had succeeded in writing a play, essay, history or philosophical treatise of generally acknowledged merit. But when it came to novels women had already triumphantly demonstrated their ability to compete successfully with their brother novelists. Mrs Radcliffe (1764–1823), Fanny Burney (1752–1840) and Maria Edgeworth (1767–1849) had all succeeded.

Finally Jane Austen (1775–1817) herself, who died only a few months after Charlotte Brontë was born, had already earned the distinction of being described by many critics as the greatest novelist of her time.

Thus for the three Brontë sisters, passionately eager for creative fulfilment, it was perfectly natural to regard the novel as offering the one reasonable and proven road to success. They all wrote poetry. Emily, in fact, wrote a small amount of noble and distinguished poetry. But this would have counted for nothing if they had not been able to employ the form of the novel to demonstrate their genius.

A note on the text

The novel first appeared as *Jane Eyre: An Autobiography,* edited by Currer Bell, 3 volumes, 1847. It was reprinted in 1847 as 'Edited by Currer Bell', with a Preface, and a Third Edition was published in 1848 with 'A Note to the Third Edition' signed by Currer Bell. This is the text used in the Penguin English Library, edited by Q. D. Leavis, Penguin Books, Harmondsworth, 1966.

Part 2

Summaries

of JANE EYRE

A general summary

Jane Eyre is a ten-year-old orphan, unwanted and neglected, in the home of her aunt, Mrs Reed. She is sent away to Lowood, a charity school for girls of good family. During her first few months she suffers greatly, as do all the girls, from hunger, cold and severe discipline. Following an outbreak of typhus the school is reformed and improved. In her eight years there Jane gains a sound education and becomes a student teacher. Then, on the retirement of the Principal, Miss Temple, to whom she is deeply attached, Jane herself resolves to leave. She is engaged to teach a single pupil in a country house, Thornfield, in the English Midlands. For three months she lives quietly in the company of her pupil, Adèle, and the housekeeper, Mrs Fairfax. Then the owner and her employer, Mr Rochester, arrives to live there for a time. Although a dominating personality he finds her interesting and treats her kindly. On two separate occasions Jane earns his respect by showing courage and determination when facing danger. She soon falls in love with him but is obliged to witness his courtship of a handsome girl of good family, Blanche Ingram, whom he is expected to marry.

Jane is summoned to attend the death-bed of Mrs Reed. She finds that an uncle, Mr Eyre of Madeira, offered to adopt her several years previously only to be informed that she died at Lowood. She has thus lost the prospect of security and independence. Mrs Reed dies and Jane returns to her job at Thornfield. Mr Rochester is still there. To Jane's surprise and delight he offers to marry her. His love for Blanche Ingram has been a pretence. The wedding ceremony, a month later, is interrupted by a lawyer representing Jane's uncle. He accuses Rochester of having a wife still living and of attempting the crime of bigamy with Jane. This charge is proved to be true. Jane has long been aware of a sinister presence in the house. This is now known to be Mrs Bertha Rochester, a mad Creole from Jamaica, caged like a wild animal in an upper floor at Thornfield. Jane is deeply shocked. Mr Rochester tries to excuse his conduct. His love for Jane has been real. He now urges her to go away with him as his mistress. She steadfastly refuses. Still loving him, but in great distress, she runs away. After a hurried secret journey she finds herself a penniless and homeless refugee in a distant part of the country. Wretched and exhausted she is finally taken to the home of two sisters and a brother called Rivers. The two girls quickly become her friends; the brother, St John, who is a country clergyman, finds her a job teaching the local girls in a simple school.

Although Jane has refused to reveal her own history St John Rivers soon finds out who she is and why she has run away. Astonishingly enough it turns out that he and his two sisters are Jane's first cousins. Their uncle who has just died is also Jane's uncle, Mr Eyre of Madeira. He has left all his wealth to Jane and none to the other three. Jane insists that it should be divided equally, and settles down to share the independent life of Diana and Mary Rivers. She is, however, distressed to hear no news of Mr Rochester whom she still loves. Meanwhile St John is preparing to travel to India as a Christian missionary. He urges Jane to marry him and join in his missionary service. She is willing to serve but not to marry him. There is a long clash of wills. When finally in danger of yielding to St John's unfair pressure, Jane hears a strange unexplained call for help in the voice of Mr Rochester. Without hesitation she leaves the Rivers home, returns to Thornfield, finds that it has been destroyed by a fire in which Bertha Rochester has died and Mr Rochester has been blinded and seriously injured. Jane does not rest until she finds him in another of his country homes. They are happily reunited. He is now free to offer her honourable marriage in which they both find great happiness.

Detailed summaries

Chapter 1

Jane opens her story as a ten-year-old orphan in the home of her uncle's widow, Mrs Reed, of Gateshead Hall. Her cousins, Eliza, John and Georgiana Reed, are fondly treated, while Jane is made to feel unwanted. Mrs Reed tells her, quite unfairly, that until she can be more frank and sociable she cannot be accepted on her cousins' terms. She seeks refuge in a book in the next room, and is happily absorbed in it until she is dragged out by John, an unhealthy fourteen-year-old who delights in tormenting her. Terror, for once, drives her first to complain and then to resist him. John is surprised and accuses her of attacking him. Mrs Reed condemns Jane to be locked up in a spare bedroom, known as the 'red room'.

NOTES AND GLOSSARY:
The many geographical and literary references are unimportant in themselves, but they are an immediate indication not only of a ten-year-old's high intelligence but also of her astonishingly powerful imagination.

There are no concessions to childhood in Jane's narrative style, which is fully adult, coming from a woman of thirty, not a child of ten.

Notice also her capacity for reasoning analysis in her account of her cousin John.

moreen: thick patterned material
Madam Mope: nickname implying that Jane is sulking

Chapter 2

Jane is forcibly removed to the red room by Bessie and Abbot, but escapes being actually tied up by promising not to move. Left alone she puzzles over the injustice of her treatment and is distressed to realise that she is a total outcast. Then, as it grows darker and colder, she recalls that she is in the room her uncle, Mr Reed, died in. She fancies that his spirit may return. Utterly panic-stricken she screams to be let out and shakes the door. The servants return in some concern, but Mrs Reed herself arrives to confirm her original cruel sentence. Jane is locked in once more, has some kind of fit and loses consciousness.

NOTES AND GLOSSARY:
Jane's imagination, sensitivity and powerful emotions are all again in evidence.

The two servants think it would be quite a normal course of action to tie her to the chair.

Abigail: a lady's maid
with so much cover: with so much of an unknown quantity
tabernacle: a tent, shrine
Marseilles counterpane: a heavy patterned cloth
indemnity: forgiveness
pea-chicks: the young of peacocks, ornamental birds

Chapter 3

Jane wakes up, as if from a nightmare, in the comfort of her own bed. Bessie, more sympathetic than before, and a visitor, whom Jane recognises as Mr Lloyd the apothecary, are there. He speaks kindly to her but soon departs. Jane passes the night in fear and wakefulness. Next day she gets up but is still deeply affected, weak and miserable. Bessie tries to treat her more kindly. Mr Lloyd calls and spends some time questioning Jane. Although he fails to comprehend the full extent of her misery he takes the trouble to recommend to Mrs Reed that it would be sensible to send her away to school. Mrs Reed is very ready to adopt this suggestion.

Jane learns, through Abbot, that her mother was disinherited for marrying a poor clergyman, her father, and both died in poverty while Jane was still a baby. Abbot and Bessie agree that they could have felt more sympathy for Jane if she had been a less unattractive child.

NOTES AND GLOSSARY:

A great deal of our assessment of Jane's character springs from the honest and direct way she talks in the various dialogues.

physician:	a doctor of superior status
ghastly:	haunted
fagging:	carrying out dull tasks
laid out:	prepared for burial
caste:	used (incorrectly) by Charlotte Brontë to mean social rank
in the stocks:	in a punishment frame that grips the ankles or legs
backboards:	stiffeners for the back or spine
net:	knit
Guy Fawkes:	a man (1570–1606) who tried to blow up the Houses of Parliament, was tried and hanged

cut her off without a shilling: disinherited her

Chapter 4

Jane enters upon a period of frustrated hope and expectancy, during which time her outcast state is confirmed. She stands up against Mrs Reed for the first time, somehow finding the courage to deny the accusation that she is unfit to associate with her cousins. After nearly three months, including the festival of Christmas from which she is totally excluded, she is summoned by Mrs Reed to meet the Principal of Lowood School, Mr Brocklehurst. He asks questions and lectures her. Jane is distressed when Mrs Reed accuses her of being deceitful. She thinks this will ruin her prospects before she even arrives at the school. When Mr Brocklehurst has gone, agreeing that Jane should be sent, as soon as possible, Jane's outraged sense of justice is too strong for her, and she bursts out in indignant self-defence. She addresses Mrs Reed with such uncontrollable passion and fervour that, so far from being punished, she actually wins a moral victory over her. Mrs Reed is alarmed and subdued, relieved to think that Jane will soon be away. Jane receives a little comfort from Bessie, the only person in the Reed household to regard her with any warmth or affection.

NOTES AND GLOSSARY:

A powerful sense of right and wrong develops in Jane. There is more bluntness and directness in the dialogue. A feeling of fulfilment and triumph follows Jane's victory over Mrs Reed. She is to be one of life's fighters and she has just won her first battle.

corruption:	*(in this instance)* outburst
traffic:	*(in this usage)* bargaining, buying and selling
sable-clad:	dressed in black
ruth:	*(archaic)* pity
'sotto voce':	*(Italian)* in a low voice
'onding on snaw':	*(Yorkshire dialect)* about to snow

Chapter 5

Long before daybreak on a midwinter day Jane is despatched by stage coach on the fifty-mile journey to Lowood. Arriving in the dark after a wearisome journey she is kindly greeted by Miss Temple, the superintendent. She entrusts her to Miss Miller, an assistant teacher. Jane is plunged into the austere, severely disciplined life of a charity girls' school. After a short night's sleep they all get up very early on a bitterly cold morning. After prayers and Bible readings the simple breakfast proves to be inedible because the porridge is burnt. The day's timetable consists of more lessons, compulsory outdoor exercise and inadequate meals. Jane talks to a girl called Helen Burns, and finds out that Miss Temple is generally loved and respected, but is unable to counteract the meanness of Mr Brocklehurst. Later Jane is surprised to observe Helen Burns submit, apparently quite calmly, to a humiliating punishment.

NOTES AND GLOSSARY:
This chapter is based largely on Charlotte Brontë's recollections of her own early months at Cowan Bridge.

Notice the 'abruptness' of the dialogue between Jane and Helen Burns, two intelligent girls using language with straightforward accuracy to represent clearcut thinking.

dips:	rough candles
inanition:	emptiness (here of the stomach)
organ:	*(in this instance)* part of the mind
irids:	irises, the coloured parts of eyes
front:	used by Charlotte Brontë to mean 'forehead'
'Rasselas':	a novel by Dr Johnson (1709–84), the famous lexicographer, poet and critic

Chapter 6

The following day is much colder. The girls are unable to wash in the morning as the water is frozen. Jane starts normal school-work, disliking the practice of learning lessons by heart. Later in the day, while sewing, she observes her new friend, Helen Burns, as one of a class being taught history by Miss Scatcherd. Despite her mastery of the subject she is repeatedly, and Jane thinks unfairly, rebuked by Miss Scatcherd. Eventually she receives a painful beating on the neck and shoulders. In the evening Jane manages to hold a further conversation with her. Feeling herself that injustice and oppression must be resisted Jane cannot understand Helen's belief in the doctrine of Christian forgiveness and endurance.

NOTES AND GLOSSARY:
Helen preaches the orthodox Christian lessons of forgiveness and meekness. Jane, the fighter, despite the attraction Helen Burns has for her, is most reluctant to be passive, to endure without resistance.

Charles I:	English king (1625–49) defeated and then beheaded
poundage and ship-money: taxes charged by Charles I	
licensed uproar:	a loud noise that is permitted
Felix:	*(biblical)* a figure in the New Testament of the Christian Bible

---

Chapter 7

Jane's first three months at Lowood are hard to endure, with the ills and pains of a severe winter added to the almost prison-like existence with its poor food and routine labour. After three weeks Mr Brocklehurst visits the school and lectures pupils and staff, including Miss Temple, on the moral virtues of grim poverty, unrelieved by any natural pleasure. The hypocrisy of his attitude is underlined by the luxury and extravagance displayed in the dress and style of his wife and daughters who accompany him. Observing Jane he cruelly singles her out to be condemned as a 'liar' who has been unfit to live in the 'benevolent' Reed household. Jane is inspired to endure this injustice by her awareness of Helen's sympathy.

NOTES AND GLOSSARY:
Notice the power of money. Mr Brocklehurst is quite ready to bully Miss Temple, as well as the girls, because she is a paid employee.

Notice the violence of Charlotte Brontë's hatred of evangelism and hypocrisy when they are joined in one character like Mr Brocklehurst.

Notice also the angelic quality of Helen Burns.

quarter:	an academic term
Eutychus:	*(biblical)* a young man who was restored to life by Paul after falling from a housetop

'en masse':   *(French)* all together
surtout: *(originally French)* a long overcoat
brand: put on a mark that cannot be removed
false front: a fringe of artificial hair
the Rubicon was passed: there was no going back, the phrase coming from Julius Caesar's (102/100 BC–44BC) crossing the river Rubicon with his troops after the Roman Senate had ordered him to resign his command; this led to his victories over the Senatorial armies and to his becoming dictator
Brahma and Juggernaut: Hindu gods
Bethesda: *(biblical)* a pool of healing water
effluence: literally 'outflowing', here it means a radiation over the face

Chapter 8

Jane has been overwhelmed by the shame to which Mr Brocklehurst has exposed her. Helen Burns tries, not very successfully, to comfort her by preaching Christian meekness. Both girls are then invited to Miss Temple's room where Jane is given the chance to tell her own story of Gateshead. Miss Temple undertakes to seek Mr Lloyd's confirmation of it. Later Jane is astonished to listen to the wisdom and learning that Helen Burns reveals in conversation with Miss Temple. When the two girls leave Jane notices Miss Temple's tender concern for Helen. About a week later Miss Temple hears from Mr Lloyd and Jane is relieved to be publicly cleared of the accusation laid against her by Mr Brocklehurst. Thus encouraged she sets about her work with renewed interest and vigour, realising that she now has good reason to prefer Lowood, for all its hardships, to the more comfortable home of the Reeds at Gateshead.

NOTES AND GLOSSARY:
Miss Temple, of course, realises that Helen Burns is seriously ill, and likely to die quite soon. Jane now faces life at Lowood with determination and enthusiasm.

Virgil: Publius Vergilius Maro (70–19BC), Latin epic poet, author of the *Eclogues,* the *Georgics* and the *Aeneid,* commonly studied by schoolboys, less commonly by girls
phylactery: a religious charm, worn on the forehead
'être':   the French verb 'to be'
Barmecide supper: an imaginary feast (from the *Arabian Nights)*
Cuyp: Albert Cuyp (1620–91), Dutch landscape painter

Chapter 9

With the coming of spring and May, Jane becomes aware of the natural beauty around Lowood. The mild weather leads to an epidemic of a dreaded disease, typhus. Many girls die; others are removed, possibly to die at home. The institutional timetable is abandoned and paradoxically life becomes much easier for the minority still healthy. Jane is one of these, but she finds that Helen, although unaffected by typhus, is dying in Miss Temple's room of quite a different disease, consumption, as pulmonary tuberculosis was then known. In her anxiety to see Helen again Jane makes her way there late at night. Helen, although very weak, tells Jane that she is happy in the Christian expectancy of a life to come. Jane is unable to share her faith. She lies down with Helen and the two girls fall asleep in each other's arms. In the morning Jane awakes only as she is being carried away from the bed on which Helen has died.

NOTES AND GLOSSARY:

Charlotte Brontë is medically incorrect about typhus. It is not due to a 'fog and fog-bred pestilence' but is a louse-born disease. The epidemic of typhus at Lowood is caused by the unhappy fact that most of the girls cannot help being lousy. It is thus due more to a lack of hot water and washing facilities than to the climate. Charlotte Brontë is quite correct, however, to say that the girls are easy victims because they are underfed and ill cared for.

Remember that Helen Burns dies of a completely different disease, pulmonary tuberculosis, of which coughing – especially coughing blood – is the principal symptom.

The significance of the 'fifteen years' is that Jane herself must have returned to order the memorial tablet four or five years after her marriage to Rochester.

Canadian:	here refers to many degrees of frost
auriculas:	spring flowers, as are the others mentioned
'ing' and 'holm':	two more north country words meaning stretches of land in, or alongside, water
'Resurgam':	*(Latin)* 'I shall rise again'

Chapter 10

Eight years of Jane's life at Lowood are passed over very quickly. After the serious epidemic of typhus the conditions at Lowood are found to have been very defective. A new building is put up and the school restarted under a kinder management and along more generous lines. Jane relates how she spent six further years there as a pupil, working her way up to the head of the school, and then became a young teacher for two more years. As long as Miss Temple remains Jane is content to work hard and improve, but when Miss Temple leaves to get married Jane immediately feels restless and restricted. She decides to advertise for a job as governess, receives an offer from a household seventy miles to the south, and finally arranges to leave Lowood to take up this new post. On the eve of her departure she receives an unexpected visitor from Gateshead Hall, the maid Bessie. She brings news of the Reeds, of how the two sisters quarrel, the son John has failed his law examinations, and the mother is worried by his extravagance. She also relates how Jane's uncle, a respectable-looking man from Madeira, called to inquire after Jane seven years previously.

NOTES AND GLOSSARY:
Jane's lively spirit, having been happily subdued under Miss Temple, is suddenly aroused as soon as she departs. Her plans are all her own; she seeks advice from no one. Bessie admires Jane's 'lady-like' skills – in music, painting, needlework and French.

debarrassed:	relieved
'en règle':	*(French)* in the correct way
plucked:	*(slang)* failed by the examiners

Chapter 11

After a long cold journey by stage coach Jane arrives at the town of Millcote. Thence she is brought by carriage to Thornfield, arriving in the evening. She is kindly welcomed by Mrs Fairfax who has employed her and who seems to be the mistress of the house. In the morning Jane finds out that the real owner of Thornfield is a gentleman called Rochester who is usually away from home. Mrs Fairfax, although distantly related by marriage, is no more than the housekeeper. Jane meets her pupil, a French girl of seven or eight called Adela (or Adèle in French) Varens. She compliments Jane on the excellence of her French pronunciation. Mrs Fairfax shows Jane the house. It is almost empty but living in the top storey there is a woman called Grace Poole, whose conduct strikes Jane as rather mysterious.

NOTES AND GLOSSARY:
The status of Thornfield is clearly stated to be 'a gentleman's manor house, not a nobleman's seat'. It is not a castle or splendid house but is nevertheless the largest dwelling house in the neighbourhood.

Notice the first encounter with Grace Poole and the first association of her and the extraordinary laughter.

Wolfe:	James Wolfe (1727–59), an English general who captured Quebec, and died in the hour of victory

'boots': an inferior servant at an inn or hotel whose normal job was cleaning boots and shoes

Quaker-like: in the style of the Quakers, a Christian sect that avoided all luxury

cuirass: a part of old body armour covering back and chest

the etymology of the mansion's designation: how the house got its name

'C'est la gouvernante?': *(French)* 'Is that the governess?'

'Mai oui, certainement': *(French)* 'yes indeed'

canzonette: a light, brief song

'La Ligue des Rats': *(French)* a fable, or animal story

'Qu'avez-vous donc?': *(French)* 'What's the matter?'

'lui dit un de ces rats': *(French)* 'one of these rats said to him'

'parlez!': *(French)* 'speak!'

Tyrian-dyed: dyed a rich purple

Parian: a kind of Greek marble

'Mesdames, vous êtes servies!': *(French)* 'Ladies, dinner's ready!'

'J'ai bien faim, moi!': *(French)* 'I'm very hungry, I am!'

Chapter 12

Jane quickly settles down to life at Thornfield becoming friendly with Mrs Fairfax and Adèle. Although comfortably settled she is often restless and stirred by a desire for something more vigorous and inspiring. She is convinced that women need action and fulfilment no less than men. After about three months, on a January afternoon when Adèle is let off school-work, Jane goes into the village of Hay to post a letter. On the way she encounters a rider whose horse falls on the icy road. She gives him what help she can; having remounted he rides off. When she gets back to the house she finds the rider's dog in Mrs Fairfax's room. The rider she has helped is her employer and the owner of Thornfield, Mr Rochester.

NOTES AND GLOSSARY:

Notice Jane's (and probably Charlotte Brontë's) professional attitude to student-teacher relationships – far from sentimental.

Notice also Jane's statement on 'women's rights' in the fifth paragraph.

Study the account of her first meeting with Rochester. The excitement makes her increasingly restless – almost unable to make herself re-enter the placid house.

'par parenthèse': *(French)* by the way

'Revenez bientôt, ma bonne amie, ma chère Mlle Jeannette': *(French)* 'Come back soon, my good friend, my dear Miss Jane'

pretercanine: having something more than doglike about them
'the mountain will never be brought to Mahomet': old saying to which the rider supplies the second part – 'Mahomet must go to the mountain'

Chapter 13

On the following evening Jane, Mrs Fairfax and Adèle are all summoned to Mr Rochester's presence. He still cannot walk because of his injured ankle. His manner is grim and unsmiling – hardly even polite. He dismisses Adèle and asks Jane for the details of her family and brief experience. It seems that he is trying to frighten her but she is quite unmoved by his autocratic manner, confessing that she might have been more embarrassed if he had been kinder and gentler. He is pleased to find – and pleases Jane by telling her – that Adèle has improved. He orders Jane to play a piece on the piano and quickly decides that she is no more than a fair musician. But when he examines her paintings he discovers in them a powerful visionary quality that surprises him. He is impressed, but then tells her to take Adèle off to bed. Later in the evening Jane asks Mrs Fairfax why he seems so changeful and abrupt. Mrs Fairfax reveals that he had a distressing dispute with his father and elder brother Rowland when he was a young man. Although Mrs Fairfax is ignorant of the details she thinks that Mr Rochester's father forced him into an unfair position over money. Since inheriting the estate from his elder brother nine years before he has been a restless traveller, seldom at home for more than a few weeks at a time.

NOTES AND GLOSSARY:

In those days 'tea' was taken in the early evening *after* a still earlier dinner.

Rochester is presented from the start as a masterful character of whom Jane refuses to be afraid.

Notice Jane's professional pride. The only suggestion of Rochester's that can upset her is that she may have been helped by an art master.

prenomens: forenames
'Et cela doit signifier . . . mademoiselle?': *(French)* 'And this should mean that there will be a present inside there for me, and maybe for you too, Miss. Mr (Rochester) has spoken of you: he has asked me the name of my governess, and if she isn't a tiny person, rather thin and a bit pale. I said 'yes' for it's true; isn't it, Miss?'
Heidelberg: a university city in Germany
disembarrassed: 'calm and easy'

'N'est-ce pas, Monsieur, qu'il y a un cadeau pour Mademoiselle Eyre dans
votre petit coffre?': *(French)* 'Isn't it true, Sir, that there's a present for Miss Eyre in your little box?'

'you beat about the bush': 'you don't give a direct answer'

consoles, chiffoniers: *(French)* two specialist names for pieces of furniture

men in green: fairies

your rings: a ring was a circle of fairy magic. Rochester repeatedly suggests that Jane is a fairy

religieuses: *(French)* nuns

Latmos: mountain in Greek mythology

Chapter 14

Several days later Jane and Adèle are again invited to spend part of the evening with Mr Rochester. Adèle is delighted to receive the present she has been expecting. Meanwhile Mr Rochester has a long conversation with Jane. This ranges over various subjects. Being both older and the master, Rochester assumes the dominant role. Jane is frequently puzzled but her good sense and independence save her from submitting tamely to his will or opinions. She has the courage to speak the truth even when this seems to reprove Mr Rochester. He is clearly very impressed by her intelligence and personality. Eventually she is permitted to take Adèle off to bed.

NOTES AND GLOSSARY:

In the long conversation between Jane and Mr Rochester, the man's share is difficult and challenging. Jane meets the challenge simply but successfully. This chapter hints at the growing attraction Jane has for him – notably in the reference to 'the bonny wanderer', 'the pilgrim' that has already done him good, and his statement 'my heart was a sort of *burial place* charnel; it will now be a shrine'.

Notice also ' "Let it be right" – the very words: you pronounced them'. It seems that he has already made his resolve – astonishingly quickly.

'petit coffre': *(French)* little chest

'Ma boite!': *(French)* 'My box!'

'tiens-toi tranquille: enfant; comprends-tu?': *(French)* 'Keep quiet, child. Do you understand?'

'Oh ciel! Que c'est beau!': *(French)* 'Oh heavens! How lovely it is!'

tête-à-tête: *(from the French)* private talk

auditress and interlocutrice: woman for her to converse with

preciously grim: in modern English 'precious grim' – precious meaning 'very'

'nonnette':   *(French)* a little nun
'et j'y tiens':   *(French)* 'and I stick to it'
'when you were eighteen': suggesting that she claims to be eighteen now
forte: *(from Italian)* strong point
the law of the Medes and Persians: supposed to be unalterable
like a sphinx: that is unintelligibly
'Il faut que je l'essaie! ... et à l'instant même!': *(French)* 'I must try it
                    on ... and at this very moment!'
'Est-ce que ma robe va bien? ... et mes souliers? et mes bras? Tenez, je
                crois que je vais danser!': *(French)* 'Does my dress
                look well? ... and my shoes and stockings? Wait, I
                think I'm going to dance!'
chasséed: *(from ballet language)* moved in a dance step
'Monsieur, je vous remercie mille fois de votre bonté ... C'est comme cela
        que Maman faisait, n'est-ce pas, Monsieur?': *(French)*
        'Sir, I thank you a thousand times for your
        generosity ... That's how Mamma used to do it,
        isn't it Sir?'
green: *(double meaning)* not only fresh and young but also
          easily deceived

Chapter 15

Several weeks later, while they are walking in the grounds, Rochester engages Jane in a further long conversation. He tells her of the mistress, Céline Varens, whom he maintained in luxury in Paris, and how she betrayed him. After breaking off in a grim passion to express his determination to like the Thornfield he has hated for so long, he tells Jane the rest of the Céline Varens story; how he threw her off and fought a duel with the other man; and how she finally left him an illegitimate child she alleged to be his. Rochester adopted her out of pity. He asks Jane if she would prefer not to be governess to an illegitimate orphan. Jane says she is fonder of Adèle because the child has no one else to love her.

Jane is aware of Mr Rochester's growing kindness to her and of her own response. She is happier and healthier. She acknowledges her increasing affection for him.

That night Jane hears a suspicious noise at her bedroom door, and goes in search of Mrs Fairfax. There is smoke in the passage, coming from Mr Rochester's bedroom. His bed is in flames. Jane immediately puts the fire out, using the several jugs of water ready to hand. Mr Rochester wakes up, bewildered, and confirms, as Jane thinks, that the cause of the fire must have been Grace Poole. He thanks Jane warmly for her courage and presence of mind in saving his life. In the stress of emotion he seems to be about to express a strong feeling for her. Jane returns to bed, her heart surging with her joyful awareness of his tenderness for her.

NOTES AND GLOSSARY:
Victorian readers were shocked by Mr Rochester's telling the story of his French mistress to the innocent governess. Girls in those days were not supposed to be aware of such relationships. Jane's presence of mind and courage when faced by a physical danger, such as the bedroom fire, are also unfamiliar qualities in a Victorian heroine. Notice Mr Rochester's acknowledgement of the 'delight' that struck to his 'inmost heart' when he first saw Jane beside the road to Hay.

'grande passion':	*(French)* consuming love affair
'taille d'athlète':	*(French)* physique of an athlete
Apollo Belvedere:	famous statue of ideal Greek manly beauty
Gallic sylph:	French fairy
'hotel':	*(French)* a town house or villa, *not* a hotel
'dentelles':	*(French)* pieces of lace
spoony:	*(old slang)* infatuated lover
Havannah:	Havana, where the best cigars came from
'croquant':	*(French)* crunching
'voiture':	*(French)* carriage
flame:	old slang for 'girl friend'
inamorata:	*(Italian)* a woman with whom one is in love
'porte cochère':	*(French)* carriage gateway
Job's leviathan:	*(biblical)* mythical monster in the book of Job
habergeon:	coat of mail, flexible armour
roué:	*(from the French)* wastrel or rake
'beauté mâle':	*(French)* manly beauty
encountering:	meeting in a duel
hills of Beulah:	*(biblical)* land of great happiness

Chapter 16

Although she hopes to see Mr Rochester, Jane passes the following day normally. Meeting Grace Poole, whom she presumes to have been the cause of the fire, she tries to provoke her into some admission of guilt. But the woman is quite calm, simply advising Jane to keep her bedroom door locked at night. Jane wonders what hold such an unattractive person can possibly have over Mr Rochester. In the evening Mrs Fairfax tells her that Mr Rochester has gone away on a social visit. Jane is bitterly disappointed. Mrs Fairfax describes some of the people with whom he will be staying, in particular a very beautiful and accomplished girl called Blanche Ingram. Jane tells herself she has been foolish to suppose that Mr Rochester could possibly be drawn to a poor and unattractive girl like herself. As an act of self-discipline she undertakes to produce two portraits, one of herself and a second of the supposed Blanche Ingram, as a reminder of this folly. Thanks to this determination she teaches herself not to indulge in romantic hopes.

NOTES AND GLOSSARY:
Notice the typical resolution with which Jane meets the disappointment of finding that Mr Rochester has gone away, apparently indifferent to her and possibly in pursuit of a much more beautiful and socially suitable girl.

'Qu'avez-vous, mademoiselle? . . . vos doigts tremblent comme la feuille, et vos joues sont rouges: mais rouges, commes des cerises!': *(French)* 'What's the matter with you miss? . . . Your fingers are trembling like a leaf, and your cheeks are red – positively as red as cherries!'

jetty: completely black

fortunes: dowries

'Arraigned at my own bar . . .' *(legal)* 'Accused by my own common sense . . .'

Chapter 17

During the next fortnight Jane continues trying to be level-headed about Mr Rochester, and even thinks of making a move from Thornfield. Then Mrs Fairfax receives a letter announcing Mr Rochester's return, with a large party of guests, in three days' time. The house is plunged into a frenzy of preparation. Adèle's lessons are abandoned and Jane is employed as extra household assistant. Grace Poole also assists in supervising the extra cleaners. Her strange position in the household is accepted unquestioningly by the rest of the staff, and Jane deduces that they all know something about Grace Poole's highly-paid duties that is still a mystery to her.

When the guests arrive Jane finds that she has to fend for Adèle and herself. She is quite happy to do this and would prefer to remain right out of the way, but on the second evening she is instructed to bring Adèle to the drawing room after dinner. Jane seeks a quiet corner where she hopes to be little noticed, but cannot escape some rudeness and scornful looks when the eight ladies, four elderly and four young, arrive. She describes their splendid and fashionable attire. The Dowager Lady Ingram and her two daughters, Blanche and Mary, are particularly grand in appearance and arrogant in manner. Most of the ladies, although scarcely polite to Jane, speak kindly to Adèle who thoroughly enjoys the attention she receives. When the men arrive Jane realises how much more attractive Mr Rochester is to her than any of the others. She cannot help loving him. The Ingrams recall the dislike they felt for their various wretched governesses, whom they and their mother agree to describe as incompetent, insolent and immoral. Part of their purpose in this is to humiliate Jane herself as governess to Adèle. When they turn to music Blanche Ingram and Mr Rochester are the outstanding performers, both in song and at the piano. Jane tries to shorten the unhappiness of witnessing this scene by quietly slipping away. Rochester, however, notices her departure, follows her out and speaks kindly to her before she goes to bed.

NOTES AND GLOSSARY:

This chapter reveals some of Charlotte Brontë's weaknesses, notably in the presentation of Blanche and her mother, the Dowager Lady Ingram. They represent types that Jane and her creator dislike so intensely that they become unnatural and unbelievable, in both speech and manner. Blanche, for all her haughtiness, is intelligent and accomplished. Her French is good, she is a skilful rider, an excellent pianist and singer, well-read and knowledgeable. Charlotte Brontë wishes us to understand all this in preparation for Jane's later judgement that Blanche is too petty and mean-spirited to merit her jealousy.

There seems to be some inconsistency in Mr Rochester's behaviour. He subsequently explains that the whole of his dealing with Blanche has been to arouse Jane's jealousy. If this were really true he would hardly permit himself to weaken the effect of this policy by speaking so tenderly to her at the end of the chapter. Nor, from his observation of Jane, can he seriously suppose that any further jealousy is needed than she already feels!

'passées':	*(French)* no longer fresh and up-to-date
'a moderate pipe':	there were no cigarettes. The few women – usually elderly – who smoked used tobacco pipes
laying by:	saving money
'Elles changent de toilettes':	*(French)* 'They are changing their dresses'
'Chez maman . . . quand il y avait du monde, je le suivais partout au salon et à leurs chambres; souvent je regardais les femmes de chambre coiffer et habiller les dames, et c'était si amusant: comme cela on apprend':	*(French)* 'When I was with my mother and there were guests, I used to follow them everywhere, into the 'salon' and into their bedrooms. I often used to watch the ladies' maids doing their hair and getting them dressed, and it was such fun – that's the way you learn'
abigails:	ladies' maids

'Mais oui, mademoiselle: voilà cinq ou six heures que nous n'avons pas
mangé': *(French)* 'Yes, indeed, miss; it's now five or
six hours since we had anything to eat'

back-door: an *internal* door between the part of the first floor
containing the guests' rooms and the servants'
quarters, a 'service' door

victualage: supply of food

'et alors quel dommage': *(French)* 'and then how sad that would be'

member for Millcote: Member of Parliament representing Millcote

'Est-ce que je puis pas prendre une seule de ces fleurs magnifiques,
mademoiselle? Seulement pour completer ma toil-
ette': *(French)* 'Couldn't I take just one of these
lovely flowers, miss? Just to add a finishing touch to
my outfit'

'minois chiffonné': *(French)* unusually charming features

Diana: Roman goddess of hunting, taken as a classical
feminine beauty

'trailing': this slang term is no longer used, another archaism
explained in the text

'Bonjour, mesdames': *(French)* 'Good evening, ladies'

'sparks': *(slang)* gay and fashionable young men

'père noble de théâtre': *(French)* in the style of 'a noble father' as
presented in the theatre

irids: irises of the eyes

germs of love: seeds of love

'Tant pis': *(French)* 'so much the worse'

Miss Wilsons, Mrs Greys and Madame Jouberts: all governesses
collectively

Tedo: short form of Theodore

'a sort of lever to hoist our dead weights . . .': 'a device for getting rid of
unwanted burdens . . .'

'Au reste . . .': *(French)* 'As for the rest . . .

Signior Eduardo: *(Italian)* 'Sir Edward' as in the language of opera

Donna Bianca: *(Italian)* 'Lady Blanche' in the same language

Rizzio, Mary and Bothwell: David Rizzio was the Italian secretary to
Mary Queen of Scots (1542–87), murdered by her
husband, while James Hepburn, the Earl of
Bothwell, who later kidnapped and married her,
was a figure of romantic violence and intrigue

Corsairs: Pirates, popularised by Lord Byron's poem *The
Corsair,* published in 1814

'con spirito': *(Italian musical term)* 'with spirit'

'Gardez-vous-en bien': *(French)* 'Take care of yourself'

Chapter 18

Jane continues to observe the social activities of the house party in general and the apparent courtship of Blanche by Mr Rochester in particular. She is distressed by the latter, not simply because of her own deep love for him but because it seems obvious to her that he is not genuinely attracted by Blanche. He appears to be heading towards a marriage of convention and social convenience, not one of love. Jane now explains her own lack of active jealousy for Blanche, who seems to be a young woman without any originality of spirit or of thought. In Mr Rochester's own character Jane has ceased to distinguish any fault or weakness. She loves him so entirely that he is wholly good.

One evening when Mr Rochester is away on the excuse of business, and when the whole party is feeling rather dull in his absence, an unexpected visitor arrives, seeking Mr Rochester. He is a youngish man called Mason who has come from the West Indies. He is accepted as a fellow-guest and his manner earns the approval of the young ladies, at least, although Jane typically regards his face as too feeble and characterless to be agreeable.

An elderly gipsy woman has arrived and insists on telling the young ladies' fortunes. Blanche has to be first but when she returns her manner indicates that she has not enjoyed what the gipsy has said to her. The other three young ladies all go in together. Finally the footman tells Jane that she too is awaited by the old woman.

NOTES AND GLOSSARY:

Mr Mason, so attractive and charming in the eyes of the young ladies, is repulsive to Jane – mainly because of the lack of strength and character reflected in his face.

sacques: jackets

Paynim: old word for 'pagan'

an agent or a victim of the bowstring: the bowstring was supposed to be used for strangling. An agent or a victim of the bowstring means 'either a strangler or his victim'

patriarchal days: *(biblical)* the time of the tribal chiefs such as Abraham

'She hasted, let down her pitcher on her hand, and gave him to drink': *(biblical)* a quotation from the story of Eliezer and Rebecca in Genesis, in the Old Testament

Eliezer and Rebecca: see previous note

Bridewell: name of an old London prison

Levantine of the Eastern Mediterranean – literally 'where the sun rises' (like 'Orient')

excitation: provocation

'**Voilà Monsieur Rochester qui revient**': *(French)*'There is Mr Rochester coming back'
intelligence: *(in this instance)* information
girandoles: branched chandeliers or candle-holders
'**old Mother Bunches**': old witches
'**the old gentleman**': euphemism for 'the devil'
'**vinaigrettes**': *(French)* containers for smelling salts
'**hem**': an apologetic cough to attract attention

Chapter 19

Jane finds the strange old woman waiting for her. Does she want her fortune told? Jane is cautious and expresses disbelief. The gipsy says she is 'cold, sick and silly' to resist the chance to love and be loved. The gipsy asks her what she thinks of her master's courtship of the beautiful Miss Ingram. Jane is carefully non-committal. The gipsy, incidentally, discloses the cause of Blanche's annoyance earlier in the evening – her revelation that Mr Rochester is much less wealthy than Blanche has been led to suppose. The old woman then analyses Jane's character and her conviction that Jane will always, in the last resort, be subject to 'that still small voice which interprets the dictates of conscience'.

Towards the end of this conversation the gipsy's language has become increasingly educated and refined. She is now revealed to be Mr Rochester himself who has taken less and less trouble to maintain the disguise. Jane has been bewildered by the whole episode, but realises on reflection, that she has never been totally deceived or off her guard. So she hopes that she has not been tempted into saying anything rash or immodest. However she protests that the trick has been 'scarcely fair'. She will forgive Mr Rochester but condemns his action.

She then tells him of the arrival of Mr Mason. He is shocked. The news is a serious blow to him. He states his dependence upon Jane, and she undertakes anything in her power to serve him. Using her as an intermediary Rochester arranges to see Mason privately, later in the evening.

NOTES AND GLOSSARY:
Even when involved in a position of deceit or falsity Jane continues to be protected by her own unswerving honesty.

Mr Rochester's impersonation of the gipsy is unconvincing. He obviously does not intend to fool Jane for long, and she admits that she has been distracted by thoughts of Grace Poole.

The statement concerning the 'still small voice' of Jane's conscience is the essence of the entire book. Mr Rochester has not yet realised how powerful it will be.

nichered:	*(dialect)* laughed through the nose, like the neighing of a horse
'diablerie':	*(French)* devilry, wicked conduct
blackavised:	dark-faced
doffed:	*(archaic)* taken off
'Off, ye lendings':	quotation from Shakespeare's *King Lear*, 'let me get rid of these unwanted garments'

Chapter 20

The same night Jane and all the guests are awakened by a terrifying scream. Mr Rochester persuades his guests to return to bed. Jane, having also heard a call for help, half expects to be asked to assist in some emergency action. Mr Rochester knocks at her door and says he needs her help. In a room in the third storey Mason is lying seriously injured by a knife wound, apparently inflicted by Grace Poole. Jane is instructed to bathe the wound and administer smelling salts until Mr Rochester can return with the surgeon. Her courage is severely tested during a two-hour wait, but eventually the men arrive, Mason's wound is dressed and he is sent off by post-chaise before the servants and guests are up.

At dawn on an April morning, with Mason safely out of the way, Mr Rochester has a further talk with Jane. He presents the supposedly theoretical case of a young man who has committed a serious error in his youth and now wishes to reform. Is he entitled to a second chance, even if this means 'overleaping an obstacle of custom' or 'daring the world's opinion' in order to gain new happiness and comfort with a better companion? Although she cannot fully understand him Jane is obliged to say that atonement and reform rest with God, not with a fellow-mortal. Repulsed by the severity of her judgement Mr Rochester changes his style completely to that of a hardened and worldly man. Speaking of Blanche Ingram as his probable bride he callously asks Jane if she will sit up with him on the night before his wedding day.

NOTES AND GLOSSARY:
This chapter contains the third violent incident in which Jane displays physical courage. Notice the contempt implied in the description of the guests – 'some sobbed, some stumbled' and 'the Misses Eshton were clinging about him'.

Mr Rochester *says* that he has understood Jane's attitude to right and wrong – that she would say 'No, sir; that is impossible; I cannot do it because it is wrong', but he continues to *plan* in the hope that she may weaken in her resolve.

Incidentally, it is hardly convincing that Mr Rochester is still

contemplating marriage with Blanche when he speaks of her so
mockingly.

volatile salts: sal volatile – smelling salts used to revive someone
who has fainted.

dead as a herring: *(archaic slang)* we might now say 'dead as mutton'

blossom-blanched: that is, made white by the fruit blossom on it

spue: normally spelt spew, meaning to spit out or vomit

penchant for: *(from the French)* inclination towards

strapper: *(slang)* a large-limbed girl

ladies of Carthage: Carthage was in North Africa. Its womenfolk were
presumably black-haired

Chapter 21

On the following day Jane is summoned to receive a visitor. This is the
Gateshead coachman, who has brought news of John Reed's death, of
Mrs Reed's illness and of her wishing to see her niece. Jane asks Mr
Rochester for leave of absence which is reluctantly granted. She leaves
the next morning. At Gateshead she is welcomed by Bessie, now Mrs
Leaven, and accepted rather ungraciously into the Gateshead
household by her cousins Eliza and Georgiana. She sees Mrs Reed but
the sick woman's mind is wandering and she cannot explain why Jane
has been sent for so urgently. Jane perforce settles down to a lengthy
stay at Gateshead, occupying herself as usefully as she can, and
observing the contrast between Eliza's religious routine and Georgiana's
self-indulgent laziness. When she sees Mrs Reed again her aunt is quite
sensible and can at last explain the reason for having Jane fetched. She
produces a letter, dated three years before, in which Jane's Uncle John
had asked for news of his niece, whom he wished to adopt as his heir.
Mrs Reed confesses that she told him that his niece died during the
typhus epidemic at Lowood. Jane is startled by this information but
would nevertheless be willing to forgive Mrs Reed if that lady were ready
for a death-bed reconciliation. It seems she is not, but dies with hatred in
her heart.

NOTES AND GLOSSARY:
Eliza and Georgiana are presented almost as symbolic figures. Eliza
represents the total uselessness of a routine of religious observances.
Georgiana combines equally useless gluttony and sloth – of greed and
laziness. Charlotte Brontë and Jane heartily despise them both.

Mrs Reed acknowledges the powerful effect of Jane's first outburst
against her at the beginning of the book. It was something Mrs Reed
could neither forget nor forgive, and provided her with a motive for
blocking John Eyre's intended beneficence.

Cairngorm eye:	stony eye, brownish in colour
quiz:	*(archaic slang)* a figure of fun, someone to be laughed at
opaque to tenderness:	incapable of expressing kindness or sympathy
a Gibson:	Mrs Reed was a Miss Gibson before her marriage
deglutition:	the act of swallowing

Chapter 22

After Mrs Reed's funeral Jane's return to Thornfield is delayed by her cousins' selfish demands. Eventually, after Georgiana has left for London and Eliza has completed her preparations to enter a religious house – or nunnery – in France, Jane is released. Her return journey is spread over two days; she walks the final six miles from Millcote to Thornfield. She hardly knows what to expect, as Mrs Fairfax has written of Mr Rochester's preparations for his impending marriage. She tries not to feel too happy at the thought of returning to the home of all she loves. To her surprise she encounters Mr Rochester while still some way from the house. He welcomes her kindly, although he throws in a jocular reference to Blanche as the future Mrs Rochester. Jane, for once, cannot restrain her tongue and tells him how happy she is to be back with him, where she feels her true home to be. Mrs Fairfax, Adèle and even Leah and Sophie all welcome her with pleasure and affection. Jane hopes that she will be able to retain some affectionate association with them, even after Mr Rochester's marriage has taken place. During the fortnight that follows no further obvious preparations are made for the ceremony, but Mr Rochester is invariably kind and cheerful, even when Jane is sad.

NOTES AND GLOSSARY:
Eliza and Georgiana are despatched to their futile destinies having served as convenient targets for Charlotte Brontë's contempt.

How does Mr Rochester happen to be in the way of Jane's quiet and unannounced return? Is it mere chance, or is there an element of presentiment in it? Jane herself has discussed the theme of presentiment in Chapter 21. This is worth recalling when you read Chapter 35.

take the veil:	become a nun
vicinage:	vicinity, that is, neighbourhood
'true Janian reply':	'answer that is characteristic of you'
Boadicea:	warlike queen of the ancient Britons
philter:	normally spelt 'philtre'
Janet:	although now a separate name this was originally a 'baby' form of Jane. He means 'little Jane'
'prête a croquer sa petite maman Anglaise':	*(French)* 'ready to devour her little English mamma'

Chapter 23

At sunset on Midsummer Eve, a fortnight later, Jane goes out to enjoy the beauty of the garden. She thinks she has escaped observation and seeks a quiet corner of the fruit garden. But in fact Mr Rochester has seen her, follows and finds her there. They discuss the future. It seems that when his marriage takes place Jane will require another job. He promises to help. There could be a post at a remote house in Ireland. At the prospect of such a move Jane's courage weakens. When he says that he will also miss her she breaks down. She cannot disguise her grief and acknowledges her devotion to him. At the same time she rebukes him for treating her as if her feelings were unimportant; she protests that her spirit and soul are the equal of his. To her surprise he accepts this and proceeds to make her a proposal of marriage. She is unbelieving and asks about Miss Ingram. He says that Miss Ingram is nothing to him, that Jane is everything. She continues to doubt his declarations of love, but is finally persuaded. The compact is sealed. He says he will 'have her and hold her'. Jane, of course, is blissfully happy, but there is something strangely grim and savage about him. The sky darkens, and a violent thunderstorm breaks over Thornfield. Mr Rochester and Jane seek refuge in the house. As they enter Mrs Fairfax is distressed to see him kissing Jane repeatedly. In the morning Adèle tells Jane that the great horse chestnut tree in the orchard has been half destroyed by lightning.

NOTES AND GLOSSARY:

The chapter starts in perfect, almost Mediterranean, summer splendour, but ends in the violence of a storm, ominously destructive. There is a great deal of irony in this chapter. For example Jane says: '. . . for you are a married man, or as good as a married man, and wed to one inferior to you – to one with whom you have no sympathy – whom I do not believe you truly love . . . I would scorn such a union . . . ' She is thinking of Blanche, but speaks more accurately than she knows of the real Mrs Rochester in the top floor of the house.

Or, again, irony of a different kind may be seen in 'There is no one to meddle, sir. I have no kindred to interfere'. She has forgotten that she has a kinsman, and does not know that he will interfere.

Notice the prophetic, wholly typical, dialogue:
    'Do you doubt me, Jane?'
    'Entirely.'
    'You have no faith in me?'
    'Not a whit.'

Search through the chapter for further examples of irony or double meaning.

Albion: old poetic name for England

sunk fence:	a 'ha-ha', a wall that is invisible from the house but which prevents cattle from entering the garden from the surrounding farmland
organ of Adhesiveness:	a joke based on the 'science', then popular, of phrenology. He simply means that Jane is naturally loyal and devoted
'one can't have too much of such a very excellent thing . . . ':	another joke based on Rosalind's 'can one desire too much of a good thing?' in Shakespeare's *As You Like It*
lady-clock:	*(dialect)* ladybird
asylum:	refuge (*not* a mental hospital)
'Mrs Dinoysius O'Gall of Bitternutt Lodge,':	an imaginary name and address as part of another — cruelly bitter — joke
Connaught:	the far west of Ireland, the name of the western province

---

Chapter 24

Jane can hardly believe her own happiness in the morning. When Mr Rochester greets her he comments on the new beauty her joy has given her. He embarrasses her by plans to give her new clothes and jewels and to provide her with other luxuries. She objects. She is determined to stay as she is, independent and self-supporting. One significant favour she has to ask is that Mrs Fairfax should be properly informed of their engagement. Jane has been distressed by the housekeeper's concern over her conduct the previous evening. Mrs Fairfax finds the news difficult to believe and advises Jane to be careful in how she behaves. Jane is ready to follow this advice. On a shopping expedition into Millcote she accepts as little as she can of the gifts he would like to lavish on her, and for the rest of the month she insists on continuing as Adèle's governess, working normally and declining to see Mr Rochester except during the evenings as has been her practice. Her desire to retain her own independence also prompts her to write to her uncle in Madeira, of whom the dying Mrs Reed spoke to her. Throughout the month of engagement Jane continues to behave quietly and properly. Mrs Fairfax obviously approves of this, and although he complains of her 'hardness' it is plain that Mr Rochester also rejoices in her spirited independence and intelligence.

NOTES AND GLOSSARY:
Notice Jane's thoroughly modern attitude to approaching marriage. She loves Mr Rochester but feels degraded at the thought of being economically dependent on him.

Jane's confession that 'he stood between her and every thought of religion ... and that she could not in those days see God for the creature of whom she had made an idol' is highly significant when we come to the moral conflict that lies ahead of her.

mustard-seed: Mr Rochester is more likely to be thinking of a mustard seed in the biblical sense as tiny but powerful, than as a Shakespearian fairy

effervesce: probably used, by mistake, for 'evanesce' meaning 'fade away'

Hercules and Samson: types of strong men, Greek and biblical

Ahasuerus: *(biblical)* the king who married Esther

station: social rank, position in society

'It passes me': *(archaic slang)* 'I can't understand it'

'How it will answer ...': How it will turn out ...'

monitress: feminine of 'monitor', that is a woman giving advice

'Oh, qu'elle y sera mal – peu confortable! ...': *(French)* 'Oh, how uncomfortable she will be there! ...'

'un vrai menteur': *(French)* 'a real liar'

'contes de fée': *(French)* 'fairy-stories'

'du reste, il n'y avait pas de fées, et quand même il y en avait ...': *(French)* 'what is more there weren't any fairies, and even if there were ...'

Danae: in Greek mythology a princess loved by Zeus, and courted in a golden shower

Stamboul: Istanbul

three-tailed bashaw: arrogant ruler or 'pasha'

'pour me donner une contenance ...': *(French)* 'to give me an appearance of being at ease ...'

tyne: *(Scots dialect)* lose

The truest love ...: this love-song was Charlotte Brontë's own writing

I hied me ...': *(archaic)* I took myself ...

pished and pshawed: made meaningless exclamations of protest

Chapter 25

On the afternoon before their appointed wedding day Jane is at home, with all preparations completed, awaiting the return of Mr Rochester from an overnight visit to some farms on a remote estate. She has had an unnerving experience and is eager for his return. She roams the gardens restlessly and then decides to go to meet him. She is soaked with rain but happy to be brought back by him on horseback. Back in the house Jane tells him of the previous night. She went to bed with all her wedding garments and veil set out and had two successive dreams, one on the theme of a disappointed love and the other of a ruined Thornfield with

Jane still unable to overtake the departing figure of Mr Rochester. After the dreams came a real and more horrifying event. A large, dark and evil-looking woman entered Jane's bedroom, examined the wedding garments, tried on the costly veil that Mr Rochester had ordered, and then tore it in two and trampled on it. When this awful figure leant over her bed, Jane, for the second time in her life, fainted out of sheer terror. When she awoke in the morning the two halves of the veil were still there to prove that all this had not been a dream. Mr Rochester is shocked by this account and explains it by saying that the intruder must in fact have been Grace Poole even if it did not look like her. However he says that Jane must spend this last night before her wedding with Adèle and Sophie, and with the door locked.

NOTES AND GLOSSARY:
The wreck of the chestnut tree symbolises the marriage between Mr Rochester and his first wife: 'the cloven halves were not broken from each other, for the firm base and strong roots kept them unsundered below . . . they might be said to form one tree — a ruin, but an entire ruin'.

The ruin of Thornfield Hall raises the presentiment theme again. Compare this description of the ruin in the dream with the description in Chapter 36.

D.V.:	*(Latin)* short for *Deo volente* — if God is willing
scathed:	*(archaic)* injured
hypochondria:	(in this case) the word has the original meaning of 'a nervous malady, tormenting the patient with imaginary fears'
blond:	a piece of simple lace made from raw silk

Chapter 26

Jane is dressed for the ceremony. Mr Rochester, all hectic impatience, urges speed, checks that preparations have been made for an immediate departure and hastens Jane to the little church. Surprisingly enough there are to be no guests, not even Mrs Fairfax or Adèle, but as they enter Jane notices two strangers in the churchyard who follow them inside. The marriage service starts and they soon reach the point where the priest is required to ask if any sort of impediment is known to exist. At this crucial moment one of the strangers, a solicitor called Briggs, intervenes to say that the marriage cannot go on, explaining that he has evidence of a previous marriage — to a woman called Bertha Mason in Spanish Town, Jamaica. The second stranger then turns out to be Richard Mason himself. He confirms that the first Mrs Rochester is still living in Thornfield Hall.

The marriage service is abandoned. Mr Rochester conducts the party back to the house and then reveals the creature, his own mad wife, who has been living for ten years in the third storey of the house under the care of Grace Poole. Many people, of course, have known of her existence but none have known her to be Mrs Rochester. Jane recognises her as the terrifying visitor to her bedroom two nights previously. Mr Rochester confesses that he has intended to commit bigamy, but no one doubts his assertion that Jane herself is completely innocent.

Mr Briggs tells Jane that he has been acting on the instructions of Mr Eyre in Madeira who received Jane's letter of about three weeks previously while Mr Mason was staying with him. He has thus learned of Jane's danger and taken urgent steps to save her, although he himself is mortally ill.

During all this time Jane herself has managed to remain calm and in apparent control of her senses. She retires to her room, gradually overwhelmed by the realisation of what she has lost. She is utterly consumed by deep grief.

NOTES AND GLOSSARY:

Now that the crucial revelation has been made we must reconsider our entire assessment of Mr Rochester himself. We now know him fairly well and we probably like him fairly well too. But he has a lot to answer for. He has encouraged Jane to fall in love with him knowing that he cannot offer her honourable marriage. He has deliberately embarked on a serious crime. Is it conceivable that he could have offered a bigamous marriage to Blanche Ingram? He protests — and I think we believe him — that he loves Jane as he certainly does not love Blanche. But his affection for Jane has not prevented him from setting out to deceive her, to cheat her innocence into a pretended marriage, and to cause her a great deal of incidental suffering in the process. There is much to be forgiven and we must beware of forgiving him as readily as Jane herself will probably do.

Incidentally, of course, many smaller puzzles are now explained: the true position of Grace Poole in the story, Mr Rochester's wanderings on the Continent and long absences from Thornfield, his frenzied expectations and desperate assertions during the period leading up to his 'marriage' to Jane.

With reference to this chapter in particular we should notice the shocking conduct of Mr Rochester in the church. His language — 'Produce him — or go to hell'. 'The devil is in it if you cannot answer distinctly . . . ' and 'No, by God! . . . ' — is as profane as the crime he is endeavouring to commit.

gray old house of God: the church
Marston Moor: a battle in the Civil War of the 1640s

Creole:	this word has been used in several senses. Charlotte Brontë probably means a native of Spanish Town, but of mixed blood
ragout:	a savoury stew; possibly used here to denote a mixed-up person

---

Chapter 27

For hours Jane stays in her room in a state of nervous exhaustion, incapable of thought. Her brain starts working again late in the afternoon. What is she to do? The answer of conscience is simple but dreadful. She must leave. She realises that her love for Mr Rochester is so great that leaving him will be worse than losing him. But she knows she must make the decision – and unaided.

She opens the door. He is outside, waiting for her. He carries her down to the library and gives her some wine and food as a restorative. She feels slightly stronger. A long conversation follows, with Mr Rochester, as usual, doing nearly all the talking. He says he intends sending Adèle away to school and taking Jane off with him to share his life elsewhere. If she refuses it must mean that she does not love him. She protests that she *does* love him but *must* refuse. He then embarks on the full story of his marriage to Bertha Mason, how he was tricked into it and rapidly disgusted by it, how he was driven near to suicide but finally decided to bring her to England where she could be secretly locked up at Thornfield while he toured Europe in search of alternative comfort. He was convinced that his marriage to Bertha Mason was no real marriage, that he was entitled to seek and take another 'wife'. After several mistresses in turn failed to satisfy him he returned to Thornfield, an embittered man, only to encounter a girl of a completely different kind, young, modest, inexperienced, innocent and fresh, but, at the same time, intelligent, independent and appealing: Adèle's governess. From their first encounter in the frozen lane he felt immediately drawn to her. It seems that he loved Jane before she learnt to love him. He learnt to regard her as his chance of salvation. He now pledges her his faith and asks for hers in return, marriage or no marriage. Although she has been deeply moved by his story Jane still finds the strength to say 'no', to reaffirm her determination to leave him. With anguish in her heart and a blessing on her lips she bids him farewell and retires to her bedroom. During a short sleep she dreams that she is visited by her dead mother who advises her to 'flee temptation'. Jane rises very early, before the summer dawn, leaves the house and walks away, in an unfamiliar direction, to a road where she may intercept a coach. She pays all the money she has with her and is borne away, still agonised by the thought that in obeying her conscience she is betraying the object of her love.

NOTES AND GLOSSARY:
Jane does not attempt to disguise the strength of her inclination to accept Mr Rochester's arguments. She *does* love him and would willingly serve him. It is only with great resolution that she clings to the certain knowledge that her conscience is the voice of what is right, of what she cannot honestly resist.

Mr Rochester describes Bertha as 'unchaste'. This must mean 'unfaithful' and presents a problem. In the early nineteenth century divorce was rare but did exist. If a wife's infidelity could be established a divorce could be achieved. We must wonder why Mr Rochester has not sought and found a similar solution to the horror of his marriage to Bertha Mason. He is wealthy enough and powerful enough to have seized the chance if it presented itself and we are left to puzzle over what seems to have been a missed opportunity.

Notice the singular beauty of Mr Rochester's description of his first meeting with Jane in Hay Lane.

inanition:	emptiness, and therefore hunger
'one little ewe lamb':	*(biblical)* one small, single prized possession
rued:	*(archaic)* regretted
tent of Achan:	*(biblical)* Achan disobeyed the commands of God in trying to hide away some treasure in his tent
upas tree:	a tree in Indonesia, reputed to poison all vegetation for miles around
Grimsby Retreat:	'retreat' was an early name for a 'mental hospital' or 'lunatic asylum'
sophistical:	fallacious – apparently true but in reality false
betimes:	*(archaic)* early, in good time
Indian Messalina:	Messalina was a Roman empress, famous for her immorality. By 'Indian Messalina' he means his wife Bertha

Chapter 28

After two days of travel Jane is set down at a place called Whitcross in Derbyshire. She walks into the moorland, spends a night in the open and then returns to Whitcross. She spends the third day in or around a village a little to the west, becoming increasingly hungry and exhausted. After another night, colder and wetter, in the open, and another day of aimless wandering she arrives late on the fourth evening at the door of a small but isolated house on the edge of the moor. She observes two educated young ladies inside and begs admittance. The old servant is unwilling to allow her into the house but a young man arrives and, seeing Jane is near collapse, insists upon her being let in. She is given food and drink and put to bed, where she immediately falls asleep.

NOTES AND GLOSSARY:

Jane does not encounter much charity or kindness during her wandering until she is actually inside the house that offers her a refuge. When we recall that all these sufferings are on top of the awful loss of happiness she has endured at Thornfield we cannot be surprised that she would be content to die.

knawn't: *(dialect)* don't know
mun: *(dialect)* must
happen three miles: *(dialect)* maybe three miles
'Da trat hervor Einer, anzusehen wie die Sternen Nacht': *(German)* 'There stepped in one who looked like the starry night'
'Ich wäge die Gedanken in der Schale meines Zornes und die Werke mit dem Gewichte meines Grimms': *(German)* 'I weigh the idea in the scale of my wrath, and the works with the weight of my rage.'
'Varry like: but give ower studying . . .': *(dialect)* 'Very likely: but do stop studying now . . .'
childer: *(dialect)* children
fand: *(dialect)* found
wor mich i' your way: *(dialect)* was very much like you

Chapter 29

After lying in bed for three days and nights Jane recovers sufficiently to get up and descend to the kitchen. She makes friends with Hannah, the servant. When the brother and sisters return she tells them something of her story and begs them to help her find work, as she has no link remaining with any home or family in England. Meanwhile it is agreed that she shall stay with them.

NOTES AND GLOSSARY:

Jane quickly recognises the characteristics of St John Rivers's conduct – the lack of any natural warmth in all that he does. She shows that she is not willing to be bullied, but she is too trusting if she thinks that her limited story will protect her identity. It will be easy for him to follow up the clue she has given away, of her connection with Lowood.

brass: *(dialect)* money
dunnut: *(dialect)* don't
mucky: *(dialect)* make dirty
kirstened: *(dialect)* christened
munnit: *(dialect)* mustn't
crater: *(dialect)* creature
of a mak' of their own: *(dialect)* of a kind of their own, unusual
threaped: *(dialect)* argued or quarrelled

Chapter 30

Jane quickly becomes friendly with Diana and Mary. All three are educated and keen to study further. Diana offers to teach Jane German. She and Mary in turn are delighted by Jane's skill as an artist. Meanwhile, as the time approaches for Diana and Mary to depart for their respective posts, St John Rivers tells Jane that the post of teacher to the Morton village girls is open to her if she is willing to accept it. Although this may prove to be a humbler job than she has known Jane agrees at once. It will at least provide her with independence.

Jane observes the arrival of a letter for the Rivers family. An uncle of theirs has died leaving them virtually nothing of the money their father had led them to hope they might inherit from him. They are depressed but resolve not to despair.

NOTES AND GLOSSARY:
The sermon preached by St John Rivers gives a fair idea of his religious beliefs. He is a harsh and unforgiving follower of John Calvin, founder of a particularly severe Protestant sect. He is unsatisfied by his life as a country parson in Morton. He is planning to devote himself to missionary service in the East. Diana and Mary realise that they may be approaching 'a parting for life' and may never see him again.

Chapter 31

A few days later Jane is at her new cottage, having just completed her first day of teaching the village girls of Morton. Most of them have been rough and illiterate and she can hardly regard the future with any optimism and cheerfulness. She tries to count her blessings, and tells herself that she is better off honestly poor in Morton than if she had become a pampered mistress in Marseilles. St John Rivers visits her with a leaving present from his sisters. He advises her to be resolute and tells her something of his own struggle to accept the fate of a clergyman. He is now determined to give up all else in order to become a missionary in the East. Another visitor, Rosamond Oliver, daughter of the local landowner and industrialist, calls. In addition to being a considerable heiress she is very attractive. She obviously likes St John Rivers and encourages him to visit her home. He refuses; as a missionary he cannot afford to be attracted to a beautiful, worldly girl like Rosamond.

NOTES AND GLOSSARY:
Most of the names in this book are carefully chosen. Rosamond has the original meaning of 'rose of the world'. She is an earthly beauty. St John Rivers, the 'divine', must reject her as such.

sanded floor:	the floor was probably of brick with a sprinkling of sand over it
Lot's wife:	*(biblical)* she looked back at the destruction of Sodom and was turned to salt
Peri:	a fairy
S————:	almost certainly Sheffield, a city in South Yorkshire already famous for its steel blades
the riots:	outbreaks of machine-breaking, mainly between 1812 and 1818, protesting against over-mechanised industry

Chapter 32

Jane finds her job increasingly rewarding and enjoyable. She becomes generally well-liked by her girls' parents, but continues to grieve over Mr Rochester. St John Rivers visits the school daily to give religious instruction and Rosamond Oliver often calls as well, especially when he is there. He continues to resist her charms. Jane starts painting a portrait of Rosamond. She also visits Rosamond's home where her father expresses approval of Jane's good work at the school. After two months' work there is a holiday on 5 November. Jane settles down to complete Rosamond's portrait. St John calls with a present, a book of verse. Jane asks him how he likes the picture and if he would like a copy. He explains his conviction that Rosamond Oliver would not make him a suitable wife; there would be no point in his possessing her portrait. In covering Jane's painting his eye is caught by some kind of mark on the protective paper. To Jane's surprise he tears this off, pockets it and leaves her.

NOTES AND GLOSSARY:

St John Rivers is quite disconcerted to be spoken to so boldly and bluntly. He acknowledges that Jane is *original*. There is something brave in her spirit.

'lusus naturae':	*(Latin)* a freak of nature or prodigy
Schiller:	a German poet (1759–1805)
miniature:	very small portrait
Mammon:	God of money or materialism
'Marmion':	epic poem by Sir Walter Scott, first published in 1808. The description of this gift as 'a new publication' is a key factor in the debate over 'dating' *Jane Eyre*
'you missed your epithet':	that is you have used the wrong adjective
'Cui bono':	*(Latin)* What good would it be?
'that caps the globe':	*(local dialect, as Jane says)* 'that's the giddy limit' or 'that beats everything'

Chapter 33

Jane is surprised that St John Rivers should force his way through the snow to visit her again in the evening. He has important news, which he introduces by relating the story of an orphan child, soon identifiable as Jane herself. He knows of her service at Thornfield and of the attempted bigamous marriage. It seems that, ever since, the solicitor Mr Briggs has been trying to locate her. She has been left the entíre fortune of Mr Eyre of Madeira, twenty thousand pounds. Jane appears to be more shocked than jubilant. She suspects that there is more to tell. St John is eventually driven to concede that he and his two sisters are Jane's first cousins; that they in fact had hoped for a share of Mr Eyre's property. Jane's reaction to this news is one of immediate delight. She is no longer alone in the world. She can see that the twenty thousand pounds is enough to be equally shared among the four of them. Diana and Mary must be called home. St John's objections are brushed aside. Within a few weeks Jane's wishes become law, the fortune is legally divided and transferred. St John, Diana, Mary and Jane herself each becomes the owner of five thousand pounds.

NOTES AND GLOSSARY:
This chapter contains much of what little humour there is in *Jane Eyre*. Even the normally humourless St John makes a joke and actually laughs. There is much humour in the conversation that reveals their clashing interests – Jane's anxiety to get news of Mr Rochester conflicting with St John's determination to concentrate on the affairs of Mr Briggs the lawyer.

Notice the rapidity with which Jane infers the chain of relationship implicit in the name Eyre, and of the tempestuous authority that determines the distribution of the legacy. St John thinks she is ill simply because he has previously never encountered a feminine will more vigorous and authoritative than his own.

Five thousand pounds was, in those days, a substantial sum – enough to make a young lady independent for life.

snuffed:	made the candle burn more brightly by trimming the wick
adverted:	referred
'Medusa had looked at you':	in Greek mythology Medusa was one of three sisters, the Gorgons. Any mortal looking at them was turned to stone
'Oh, a trifle':	this is the only joke St John ever makes
competency:	a small capital sum providing an adequate income

Chapter 34

Shortly before Christmas Jane closes the Morton school and enjoys making gifts to her many pupils. St John is surprised that she is content to give up a job she has done so well, but Jane is conscious of the need for other fulfilments. With the help of Hannah she embarks on a comprehensive cleaning and refurbishing of Moor House in order to welcome Diana and Mary home for Christmas. The three girls are delighted to share in the happiness of their new-found independence, but St John is out of sympathy with them. When Christmas is over and they all settle down to a permanent existence at Moor House he starts to exert an increasingly oppressive influence over Jane. He does not, as he promised, treat her as a sister. Instead he seems to regard her as a disciple or trainee for some hard life ahead. He himself is studying Hindustani and finds an excuse to persuade her to start studying it too. She becomes increasingly unhappy. She has failed to get any news of Mr Rochester, and finds herself becoming unnaturally submissive to St John's will, which is entirely selfish. This continues into May when St John proposes that Jane should accompany him to India as his missionary-aid. Jane is shocked but, believing that she must give up all hope of Mr Rochester and feeling in any case depressed and weak, she reluctantly consents to go with St John as his sister or curate. He rejects this and insists that she must go as his wife. He does not pretend that he loves her. He would regard her as devoted to God but married to him as part of her missionary service, and suggests that love might follow marriage. Jane summons up the strength to reject this proposal, and tells him that she scorns his idea of love, and scorns him for offering it. He is bitterly resentful but still hopes to overcome her resistance. He shows coldness and inflexibility towards her attempt at a reconciliation.

NOTES AND GLOSSARY:

During this chapter St John has developed into an increasingly overbearing and selfish character. Note the parallel between his behaviour now and that of Rochester nearly a year previously. Driven on by his passionate desire to gain possession of Jane as an earthly companion Rochester was prepared to cheat her and commit an offence against the law. Now in his equally passionate desire to gain possession of Jane as a spiritual companion St John is prepared to be equally ruthless in denying her right to earthly comforts and reasonable prospects of a happy, healthy life. Both have been prepared to be entirely unscrupulous in achieving their ends, and both have been indifferent to her welfare.

Jane seems to be in greater danger of submitting to St John *for the wrong reasons* than she ever was to Mr Rochester whom she loved more dearly. We are relieved when she expresses her scorn for St John's proposal, but are inclined to regret the apology she makes immediately afterwards.

'paysannes':	*(French)* country girls
'Bäuerinnen':	*(German)* country girls
'beau-ideal':	*(French)* perfect example
'carte blanche':	*(French)* unlimited power, full permission
Caffre:	old spelling of Kaffir
drawing away:	*(dialect)* approaching death
I know no medium:	I don't know any middle way or compromise
another slumber:	death, the normal expectation of most early nineteenth-century missionaries in India
East Indiaman:	ship sailing to India and the East (by way of the Cape of Good Hope)
him of Macedonia:	*(biblical)* figure in a vision of Paul
Demas:	*(biblical)* one of Paul's assistants who left him

Chapter 35

St John delays his promised departure for Cambridge and while he remains at Moor House Jane is miserably unhappy. She offers him a renewal of her friendship; he coldly pretends this is unnecessary. He still cannot accept her refusal of his offer of marriage. She tells him bluntly that, so far from loving her, he has almost begun to hate her. He is indignant and maintains that she is in honour bound to go to India. She denies this. She has done no more than offer to go as his companion. If he rejects this her obligation ceases. Jane is tortured by this dispute. Diana supports her and says that St John is mad to try to take her to India in any capacity.

Later in the day, he makes a fresh attack on her resistance. This time he employs a sort of religious hypnotism. Jane is on the point of yielding when she is checked by an extraordinary supernatural call for help, in the voice of Mr Rochester himself. She immediately responds, regaining her spirit and will from St John.

NOTES AND GLOSSARY:

Diana and Mary love and honour Jane. It seems surprising that they should feel so little inclined to intervene on her behalf when she is under such unfair pressure from St John.

We are thankful when Jane tells us that it is *her* time to assume ascendancy. St John's last act in her presence is to 'obey at once'. She is herself again, but she has had a narrow escape.

Dives:	*(biblical)* the rich man who died in torment
hierophant:	priest, expounder of the scriptures

Chapter 36

Next day St John leaves early. He has written Jane a note, but she is already preparing for her own journey, which takes thirty-six hours. She leaves her box at an inn two miles from Thornfield and hastens over the fields, only to find the house an abandoned ruin, evidently destroyed by fire. She returns to the inn and hears the full story from the innkeeper. In the previous autumn, the house was set on fire by Bertha Rochester. In his brave efforts to save the household Mr Rochester himself was injured, losing a hand and his sight. His wife perished. Mr Rochester is now living in seclusion in his other home at Ferndean, thirty miles away. Jane immediately engages a private carriage to take her there.

NOTES AND GLOSSARY:
The first fire described started in Mr Rochester's bed and was put out by Jane. In the second fire the bed that had been used by Jane was kindled.

Paul and Silas' prison: at Philippi, in northern Greece. It was opened by a heaven-sent earthquake
tideless sea of the south: the Mediterranean

Chapter 37

Jane arrives at Ferndean towards dusk. She sees Mr Rochester, blind and almost helpless, at the doorway. She knocks and makes her presence known to Mary and her husband John who are looking after him. Jane then enters the sitting room and tells Mr Rochester she has returned to look after him. He is overjoyed but incredulous. They spend the next day together. When she tells him about Marsh End he is curious about St John Rivers. Jane tells him that St John is young, handsome, well-educated and well bred, and Mr Rochester becomes almost absurdly jealous. Jane cannot play on this emotion and quickly reassures him that she loves him totally and no one else. Their declarations of love are exchanged again and with no barrier to their marriage now remaining this is arranged to take place without delay. Mr Rochester realises how truly blessed he is to have been checked in his first attempt to sully Jane's innocence, for now, less than a year later, he is in a position to offer a true union. He tells Jane that the call for help that she heard, when on the point of submitting to St John, really came from him and that he furthermore heard her response, the words she actually uttered, that she was coming to him. They are both struck afresh by the power and wisdom of God.

NOTES AND GLOSSARY:
The teasing humour of the conversation about St John Rivers shows

how quickly Rochester and Jane are restored to their loving sympathy.
Jane is born to serve and to give. In many ways she is now happier than
she ever was during the summer of their first, guilt-haunted courtship.
Now she can give ungrudgingly to the man she loves and whose
consuming need for her will provide her with a completely fulfilling job.
She can think of nothing better.

sightless Samson:	*(biblical)* Samson was the strong man of the Israelites, captured and blinded by the Philistines
lameter:	*(dialect)* cripple
rehumanize:	turn back into a human being
'faux air':	*(French)* misleading appearance
Nebuchadnezzar:	*(biblical)* King of Babylon who was punished by being forced to eat in the fields
cicatrized:	scarred
Saul and David:	*(biblical)* David played on the harp to help King Saul back to sanity
redd up:	*(dialect)* tidied up
'Jeune encore':	*(French)* still young
Apollo and Vulcan:	in Greek mythology Apollo was the sun god, an ideal of manly beauty, while Vulcan in Roman mythology was blacksmith of the gods
fillip:	*(here)* a flick of the finger

Chapter 38

They are married quickly and quietly. Diana and Mary send heartfelt
congratulations. St John never does, and no subsequent letter from him
refers in any way to Jane's marriage. Adèle is taken away from the
remote school where she is unhappy. More suitably placed nearby she
grows into a pleasant girl, always attached to Jane and her family.

Writing ten years later Jane describes her marriage as one of complete
happiness and mutual trust. After two years of marriage Mr Rochester
recovers much of the sight in his better eye, and regains independence of
normal movement. We also hear that Diana and Mary are both happily
married in due course. St John Rivers has continued his missionary
service in India and, after ten years, is said to be drawing near to the
'incorruptible crown' of death in Christian service.

NOTES AND GLOSSARY:
There have been plenty of indications throughout the book of Jane's
ardently passionate nature. Her final description of herself as being
'bone of his bone and flesh of his flesh' could only come from a wife
whose fulfilment lay in a fiery fusion of body and soul with the man of
her heart.

Modern readers may be surprised that the book ends not only with St John Rivers in India but with a more generous tribute to his greatness and nobility than we can readily feel he deserves.

There is no hint, apparently, that Ferndean ceases to be their home or that Thornfield is rebuilt. As Mr Rochester once said that Ferndean was too unhealthy a place in which to lock up his first wife, whom he detested, it seems surprising that he should be ready to settle down there to married life with his second, whom he adores. We are simply assured that, wherever their home is, they are entirely happy.

pulled his forelock: made a simple form of salute

she's noan faàl: *(dialect)* she's no fool

i' his een: *(dialect)* in his eyes

Greatheart: one of the nobler figures in John Bunyan's (1628–88) *The Pilgrim's Progress* (1678)

Apollyon: evil spirit or fiend, also occurring in *The Pilgrim's Progress*

exaction: performance of a demand

Part 3

Commentary

Literary aspects

Structure

The form of *Jane Eyre* has been dictated by its theme, and in the pursuit of her theme – the emancipation and development of a free woman's spirit – Charlotte Brontë is consistent and undeviating. If the form is entirely simple and straightforward this does not mean that the book lacks structure.

Style

It is less easy to defend Charlotte Brontë's prose style from some adverse criticism. The book can, at times, be fairly hard reading. Much of this is due to the author's unnecessarily laboured choice of words and grandiose expressions.

She writes of John Reed's 'spacious visage' when she means 'fat face'; of 'evacuating the refectory' for 'leaving the dining room', and prefers obscure words like 'hebdomadal', 'surtout' and 'effluvia' to the more easily understood 'weekly', 'overcoat' and 'stink'. Another aspect of Charlotte Brontë's style that occasionally arouses affectionate amusement is her habit of asking rhetorical questions and then addressing the reader directly:

And where, meantime, was Helen Burns? . . . Had I forgotten her? . . .
Surely the Mary Ann Wilson I have mentioned was inferior to my first
acquaintance . . . True, reader, and I knew and felt this . . .

At the end of the book there is the famous line:

'Reader, I married him.'

We may regret Charlotte Brontë's occasional inflation of language, and we may laugh at her confiding manner, but too much significance should not be attached to them. Where the work itself is noble and powerful a few faults cannot seriously weaken it.

The nobility and power of her prose are unquestionable. She is complete mistress of her medium. She knows what she wishes to convey and finds precise and eloquent words in which to say it. The outstanding quality of her writing is probably dynamism. It has an irresistible forward motion and drive.

Symbolism, imagery and the supernatural

Occasionally the narrative rises above the commonplace and receives an extra infusion of poetic power. The splitting of the great chestnut after Rochester's false proposal of marriage is clearly symbolic, a portent. This is followed by the nightmare visit of Bertha Rochester to Jane's bedroom two nights before the marriage, the tearing of the wedding veil that is planned for the ceremony that will betray both the real wife and the girl falsely betrothed.

There is irony in Jane's refusal to believe Rochester's first declaration, when she says she trusts him 'not a whit'. And Jane's paintings are obviously intended to have been seen by something more miraculously perceptive than her own modest hazel eyes.

It is entirely fitting that the dramatic climax of the story should hinge on the telepathic appeal Jane receives from Rochester just in time to save her from the danger of submitting to St John. There have been plenty of well-attested examples of the same sort of 'extra-sensory' communication in real life, and the reality of Rochester's cry need not be dismissed as incredible.

Narration in the first person

The chief advantages of first person narration are that we can share immediately and fully in the thoughts and feelings of the narrator. The chief disadvantages lie in the difficulty of presenting an objective portrait. Although we can become intimately familiar with Jane's heart and mind we may regret not being given a really clear account of her outward appearance.

As readers of Jane's story we are naturally prepared to offer her our affection and admiration for the duration of the book. As teller of her own story she has to reveal with becoming modesty what will make her lovable and admirable.

We get conflicting opinions on Jane's appearance. Early on Abbot calls her 'a little toad'. There can be no doubt that she is undersized and slim to the point of thinness, and remains so all her life. In her early years, at least, she is pale and colourless — what else could she be on the Lowood diet? At Thornfield she probably improves in health. She regrets that she is no beauty but there is no hint that she is unattractive. Although her clothes are plain and simple she confesses that she prides herself on being trim and tidy. Her dresses fit neatly; she is swift and silent in movement. On the morning after accepting Rochester's offer of marriage she is so happy that we cannot be surprised at his description of her — 'blooming and smiling . . . a sunny-faced girl with the dimpled cheek and rosy lips . . . and the radiant hazel eye'.

This description could hardly be applied to a really plain or unattractive girl, not even by her lover. It seems likely, therefore, that Jane is at least slim, neat, clear-skinned, healthy, animated and blessed by a sensible expression.

The element of autobiography

The definition of autobiography is attached to the title. It thus seems to claim to be the life story of the writer. Do not be deceived by this. *Jane Eyre* is a work of fiction and the sub-title of autobiography is part of the fiction. The story is presented as recollected fact; it contains nothing that could not actually have happened; and furthermore a great deal of the material is undoubtedly drawn from Charlotte Brontë's own experience. This applies especially to the early account of Jane's life at Lowood which is based quite openly on the sufferings of Charlotte and her sisters at a real institution. And Jane is clearly a projection or re-creation of Charlotte's own heart and mind.

However the work as a whole springs from the creative imagination of Charlotte Brontë the novelist. Though there is a great deal of Charlotte in the character of Jane, once she has left Lowood for Thornfield the rest of her story and her relationships with Mr Rochester and St John Rivers are entirely fictional.

The cultural resources of the Brontë sisters

The lives of Charlotte and her sisters were more restricted and confined than we may readily understand today. For most of their working lives they lived in a house that stood by itself in a bleak situation with hills and moorland around them. They had few friends and very little social life of any kind. There was no library near them. The only books they had to read were those in the house or those they could borrow. They read and re-read these with eagerness. This meant in particular that they read and were familiar with the Christian Bible, the plays of Shakespeare, many of the poems of Byron, Shelley, Keats and Wordsworth, the essays from *The Spectator* and of Dr Johnson, and all the novels they could lay their hands on.

Apart from reading what else could they do? Obviously there was no cinema, no television, no radio and no sort of recorded sound. They hardly ever went to a theatre to see a play or to a concert to hear a performance of music. They seldom saw works of art, whether paintings, sculpture, aspects of great architecture or monumental remains, and as photography was still in its infancy when they died they saw few adequate representations of such works in books or prints.

Apart from reading, which could only occupy them for a small fraction of each day, their cultural activity had to be self-created.

They drew and painted, and they wrote. They wrote in longhand, and because paper was very expensive, they developed a strange technique of writing in miniature, a writing so small that it is almost unreadable without a magnifying glass. They also, of course, sewed, as all young women had to, and for relaxation they roamed over the moors and hillsides. Their home was a substantial house, kept very clean and tidy, but barely furnished and probably rather cold. Their life might have seemed miserably hard and comfortless; but it was not. No doubt they had to endure more than their share of hardships. They certainly had their sorrows. But the very toughness of their lives made them rich and fruitful. As a family they had intensely active imaginations, passionate ambitions to fulfil their destinies and great intellectual powers to employ in their achievement.

The creation of *Jane Eyre*

Charlotte Brontë was thirty when she started writing *Jane Eyre*. She had experience of English country life, especially in the north of England, of boarding schools, educational practice and the work of a governess. She was well educated in the few subjects then available to young women, and in her case these included excellent French. She had been unhappily in love, but was still unmarried. She had had virtually no experience of the social life and manners of the aristocratic or wealthy, and had hardly travelled at all.

Most of *Jane Eyre* was written out of her own limited knowledge. When the demands of the story took her into the unknown her lack of experience was supplied by imagination. It is usually possible to tell when this has happened. For all the power and perception of her imagination she was betrayed into occasional errors of judgement or pieces of unconvincing narrative, such as the presentation of the house party with its upper-class guests at Thornfield and the episode of the gipsy fortune-teller.

The setting of the story

The whole of the story takes place in a few different parts of the Midlands and northern counties of England. These are:

Gateshead Hall, a large country house belonging to the widow of a rich landowner and magistrate, probably somewhere in Yorkshire, the county the Brontës knew best. There is plenty of evidence of wealth and size. Although there is a large household that includes many servants there are still several spare bedrooms. The fact that Jane is miserable there should not make us suppose the place itself to be unattractive or uncomfortable.

Lowood, also a large house in a country area, probably in the mountains between Yorkshire and Lancashire. Much of the building must be more like a prison than a home. Apart from a few personal apartments, such as Miss Temple's, the rooms are bare, sparsely furnished, inadequately heated and comfortless.

Lowood, however, is surrounded by beautiful, unspoilt country that can be enjoyed as soon as the iron grip of winter is relaxed. When the old buildings are condemned and the school is rebuilt in Jane's first summer and autumn it probably becomes a healthier and slightly less uncomfortable place to live in.

Thornfield Hall, another large country house nearly always simply referred to as 'Thornfield'. The church and, we imagine, a few cottages are near the house, but it is still a completely rural community, and the larger village of Hay and the town of Millcote are two and six miles away respectively. The house itself, like Gateshead Hall, is large enough to accommodate a numerous party of guests.

Moor House or Marsh End, a 'gentleman's house', would seem like a modern country cottage to us. It seems to be entirely cut off from any other human habitation. Jane's first approach is over open moorland, and there is nothing else around it.

The Teacher's Cottage, or farmhand's cottage, consisting of a single kitchen-living room below and a single bedroom above. There is no bathroom and the toilet is probably an earth closet.

Ferndean Manor, like Gateshead Hall and Thornfield, is the principal private house in its locality, being the residence of the chief landowner in the parish or village community. It is 'of considerable antiquity' and 'deep buried in a wood'.

Country life and the seasons

The action of *Jane Eyre* takes place in the English countryside, in or around six houses, or on journeys between them. It is consequently affected by the English climate and the rotation of seasons. In England, at midwinter, the days on either side of Christmas, there is not much more than six hours of broad daylight for nearly eighteen hours of darkness in every twenty-four hours. At midsummer the opposite occurs. Daylight lasts until late in the evening, and after a short night of barely six hours of darkness comes another eighteen-hour day. Temperatures also vary greatly. During the winter months of December, January and February there are frequent frosts and snowfalls, especially in the north. Even late autumn and early spring, November and March, can be very cold. On the other hand the long days and short nights of summer, in June, July and early August, are often warm, sometimes hot. The whole story of *Jane Eyre* is related to the rotation of seasons, and its events are affected by the time of the year.

Jane's first oppression occurs during a dreary November day. She has then more than two months of early winter to endure before she is sent to Lowood on 19 January, in the very depth of the English winter. Her first three months there are mainly winter, finally merging into early spring. Then comes the increasing mildness of spring in April and May. After the scandal of the typhus the reform and re-establishment of Lowood in improved buildings must have taken place in late summer and early autumn. The story resumes in August eight years later with Miss Temple's departure to be married. Jane's consequent restlessness occurs late in August, when she places an advertisement in the paper. She collects the answer early in September on a pleasant autumn day. She leaves Lowood for the last time late in October to start work at Thornfield. Then follow three quiet months of late autumn and early winter. Her walk to the post office in Hay and her first meeting with Mr Rochester when his horse falls on the ice occur in January almost exactly nine years after her first arrival at Lowood. Although Thornfield seems to be in milder country, well to the south of Lowood, conditions are still wintry enough for the causeway to be frozen hard. The first two months after Rochester's arrival at Thornfield are still winter, although the cold must be more readily endurable in a comfortable family house than in Lowood. The fire in Rochester's bedroom occurs in March. He leaves the following day, and returns with his house party in spring, March giving way to April, and plans for Easter being discussed. It is late April when Mason visits Thornfield. On the following morning, when he is packed off early after the knife attack, Jane notices that the sun is rising at 5.30 a.m. She is summoned to Gateshead at the end of the month, actually travels there on 1 May, and returns to Thornfield on an early June evening. Not surprisingly Mr Rochester is enjoying the warmth of a summer evening out of doors. The 'dubious calm' of the next two weeks culminates in the midsummer eve, warm and fragrant with a nightingale singing, when Mr Rochester makes his strange proposal of marriage. The month that passes is a time of high summer. The date of the interrupted wedding must be about 22 or 23 July. Thus the episode of Jane's flight and near-exhaustion occurs during the last week of July. She suffers greatly from hunger and fatigue, but less from cold and exposure than would have resulted at any other time of the year. The first month of her stay at Moor House is the holiday month of August, and both Diana and Mary are due to return to their separate jobs at the beginning of September. As it happens, Jane's new job, opening the

Morton school for girls, is arranged to start at the same time. St John visits her after she has had time to settle in – on 5 November, and then again on the following day, by which time there is a heavy snowfall, surprisingly early in the year even for the hilly country of North Derbyshire. The legal proceedings required to split Jane's inheritance are complete by 'near Christmas', or soon after mid-December, in time for Jane to engage in several days of cleaning and refurbishing in preparation for the Christmas holiday. Their shares of the legacy enable them to give up their jobs (as Jane also does) and they all settle down to an indefinite occupation of Moor House in the New Year and for the rest of the winter. Now that Moor House remains in occupation St John also spends part of his time there. He actually makes his first proposal in May, telling Jane that he wants her to accompany him to India when he sails on 20 June (incidentally, the first anniversary of Rochester's proposal to her). St John leaves on the morning of 1 June and Jane in the afternoon of the same day. She finds Rochester at Ferndean on the evening of 3 June, almost precisely a year after her return to him from Gateshead, and thus another anniversary. So it is full summer when Jane and Rochester are married, nearly eleven months after her escape from his attempt at bigamy in the church at Thornfield.

Jane's pride

Jane takes little pride in her social position and none at all in her possessions, which are negligible until she inherits a fortune from her uncle. She is humble about her appearance and personal charm.

She is nevertheless fiercely proud of her status as an educated and independent woman, which her conversation with Hannah at Moor House illustrates:

'Are you book-learned?' she inquired presently.

'Yes, very.'

Jane is not the sort of person to use the word 'very' lightly or unnecessarily. In the whole of her long, urgent and impassioned conversation with Mr Rochester after the broken ceremony a few days before, she does not use the word once. Yet now, when her rank as a trained intellectual is in question, she feels forced to use it. Curtly, sharply, without boasting, she is bound to say to Hannah that she is a good scholar. This flash of pride is a very human touch.

Jane's pride in her intellectual and artistic achievements is intense but not blind. For example she is aware of her limitations on the piano. She is not distressed to be described as a 'little bungler' by Rochester before he takes her place at the instrument. But she is extremely proud of her skill as an artist, and rejoices in the tributes paid to her by Bessie, Rochester, Diana, Mary and Rosamond. She takes a justifiable pride in her excellent French that earns such warm praise from Adèle. Above all she values the intellectual training and skill that enable her to match Rochester in the conflict of conversation.

Jane's attitude to social rank

It seems almost certain that the Eyres, like the Rivers and Reed families, are gentlefolk. Throughout her poverty and suffering Jane takes the gentility of her background for granted.

Even as a small child she is aware of the significance of gentle rank. Mr Lloyd asks if she would prefer to live with the Eyres if they were poor working-class people. Jane's dislike of Gateshead Hall and the Reeds cannot outweigh her distaste for poverty in a lower social class.

At Thornfield Jane is glad to feel herself to be of the same class as Mrs Fairfax – genteel in origin even if obliged by poverty to work for a living. She accepts that she is socially inferior to the Ingrams, Lynns, Dents and Eshtons, but nevertheless clings defiantly to her own independence.

When St John offers Jane the job of teacher to the girls of Morton village he and she are both aware that this could be interpreted as a degrading offer. She will be working with poor girls, cottagers' children – teaching them no more than the most elementary essentials.

Jane is deeply depressed by her first day with her twenty scholars – 'Some of them are unmannered, rough, intractable as well as ignorant'. She feels degraded. She has taken a 'step which is sinking her instead of raising her in the scale of social existence'. She tells herself that she 'must not forget that these coarsely-clad little peasants are of flesh and blood as good as the scions of gentlest genealogy', but acknowledges that this will be hard.

Jane feels unquestionably superior to servants, peasants, cottagers and the rest but she is not ill-disposed towards them. She regards the task of trying to teach the Morton girls as distasteful but meritorious. Furthermore she becomes genuinely attached to them by the end of the autumn term, and praises their progress and their manners.

Mr Rochester and St John Rivers

There are several points of similarity between these rivals for Jane. Both are dominant personalities who exert their authority to the full. Both are tempted to abuse the power that is theirs by right, whether of landed wealth or the Church. In other words each is driven to tyranny. Rochester attempts to bully Jane into a bigamous union by unfairly hiding his existing marriage. St John tries to bully her into a marriage of convenience by professing that this would be in the service of Christ.

Each deceives himself before he attempts to deceive Jane. Rochester, it seems, quite seriously believes he has been justified in his attempt to get Jane to submit to a form of marriage, because his marriage to Bertha has become meaningless in every way, physical and spiritual. St John is equally sincere in his persuasions that Jane should devote herself to the work of a Christian missionary and marry him as a token of submission.

In each case a man of conspicuous strength of character is made vulnerable to defeat because of a single weakness. It is part of Charlotte Brontë's plan to illustrate their strength, because the stronger they are seen to be the more satisfaction will spring from Jane's victories over them. For all their size, power and influence they prove to be composed of cracked metal. Jane, however puny in comparison, rings true.

Understanding the other characters

Miss Temple and Helen Burns

The only two characters in the book who are wholly idealised are female. Although Helen is made a perfect exemplar of Christian meekness we do not feel that either Jane or Charlotte Brontë herself could be equally docile. If Helen Burns had been the fugitive to Whitcross and Morton we suspect that she would quietly have lain down and died. No doubt she is an admirably pious character, but Charlotte Brontë makes Jane a fighter, less pious but more admirable than Helen.

Mr Brocklehurst

This repulsive character embodies Charlotte Brontë's detestation of the hypocrisy and cruelty that were often sadly associated with nineteenth-century evangelism.

Two sets of cousins

At the outset Jane is living with one set of first cousins, one male and two female, and towards the end of the book she settles down to life with another set of first cousins, also one male and two female. This is no accident. The contrast is intended and should be studied in all possible aspects. It is not entirely symmetrical. For example Eliza and Georgiana are entirely dissimilar and disagree, whereas Diana and Mary are alike and live in complete harmony. John and St John (the significance of the names becomes more striking when they are coupled together), although totally unlike each other in almost every way, are similar in that each seeks to impose his selfish will upon his female cousin. Both die young or fairly young, one after abandoning himself to evil, the other after dedicating himself to good.

Grace Poole and Bertha Rochester

Most readers of *Jane Eyre* will feel inclined to question whether Jane could be deceived by the Grace Poole – Bertha Rochester arrangement. Grace Poole is a tough, silent woman in early middle age who lives at the top of the house. She is supposed to be a serving woman and housemaid's assistant. But if she is no more than that why should she be obliged to live like a hermit in the third storey, away from all the other servants? Jane hears the noises made by the other, supposedly unknown, occupant of the third storey. She is told and apparently believes that all these noises are made by Grace Poole herself, who is known to be phlegmatic and silent. Jane, of course, is trusting and inexperienced, but she is manifestly no fool, and it is difficult to accept that she could be deceived in this way, especially as the stolid Grace Poole seems to proceed from one outrageous act of violence to another, the attempt to burn Rochester in his bed, the stabbing of Mason and finally the tearing of the veil. If Grace Poole had behaved so dangerously she would surely have been dismissed from the house.

The rest of the household know more. Leah, for example, knows that Grace Poole is paid more than five times her own wages for carrying out a difficult job.

Leah makes it plain that there is a secret that is not shared by the governess. She and the kitchen staff, in fact all but Jane herself, must know that enough food for two people is sent up to the third storey. They must all know that Grace Poole's arduous job, for which she is so highly paid, is that of looking after some inmate or patient. And it seems likely that this inmate must be a mental patient or lunatic.

If there has really been no suspicion of Bertha Rochester's true status, as seems reasonably possible, this must have been due more to the sheer improbability of it than to lack of gossip. On the other hand it is difficult to believe that Jane alone could be deceived for so long about the existence of a second person along with Grace Poole.

The aristocrats at the house party

It is generally accepted that the description of Rochester's guests, their conduct and conversation, is the weakest part of *Jane Eyre*. Charlotte Brontë seems to have been determined to stress the emptiness of their grandeur and ostentation. For the student the most sensible policy is simply to accept that Blanche Ingram and the rest are contributing to the development of the relationship between Rochester and Jane.

Part 4

Hints for study

This section aims to help you deal with *Jane Eyre* as an examination text.

Do not try to remember details. Examination questions seldom ask for the sort of information given in the glossaries.

Know the story as a story, how it develops and how it all fits together, linked in time and order of events.

Be prepared to explain relationships, so that you can state the connection between any one character and another, between Rochester and Mason, between Mason and Mr Eyre, between Mr Eyre and Briggs, between the Reed family and the Rivers family, and so on.

Understand, above all, that Jane's relationship with the two men who wish to marry her is the main theme. Be ready to describe and explain any aspect of this central triangle.

Types of examination questions

These usually ask you to follow one of several standard methods in dealing with the contents of the book you have studied. Of these the principal divisions are given below. Under each division are examples of the different wording that may be used to express typical questions.

(1) Recapitulation of a small part
  (a) Give an account of Mr Lloyd's conversation with Jane.
  (b) Describe the visit of Mr Brocklehurst's family at Lowood.
  (c) Give an account of Jane's first meeting with Mr Rochester.

(2) Recapitulation of selected parts
  (a) Trace the relationship between Jane and Mrs Reed from start to finish.
  (b) What part does Mason play in the development of the story?
  (c) To what extent is Jane's life at Thornfield in contact with the existence of Bertha Rochester?

(3) Dealing with a particular feature or quality
  (a) What varying opinions of governesses are expressed by different characters in the book?
  (b) How much of religious practice appears in Jane Eyre?
  (c) 'One of Jane's chief virtues is determination.' Enlarge upon this statement.

(4) Explanation
- *(a)* Explain Jane's determination to escape from Thornfield after the interrupted wedding ceremony.
- *(b)* Why is Jane angered by St John's proposal of marriage?
- *(c)* Why do you think that Charlotte Brontë makes Rochester almost totally blind for some time and then allows him to recover some of his sight?

(5) Comparison
- *(a)* Compare Miss Temple and St John Rivers as figures of moral virtue.
- *(b)* What are the chief differences between the education at Lowood and the schooling of the village girls at Morton?
- *(c)* Compare Rochester and St John Rivers in their dealings with people other than Jane.

(6) Opinion and criticism
- *(a)* 'Although small, simple and supposedly plain Jane is a truly romantic heroine.' Do you agree?
- *(b)* 'Jane Eyre is a declaration of feminine independence.' Discuss.
- *(c)* 'Although Jane and Rochester seem very different they actually have a great deal in common.' Discuss.

Methods of answering questions in the six categories are suggested in the next section.

Explanation, guidance and model answers

(1) Recapitulations of a small part

You may be asked simply to retell a bit of the story. If you know the book this should be quite straightforward, but there are still two ways in which it is easy to go wrong.

(1) Make sure that you have correctly identified the part required. This is not always easy. Suppose you are invited to give an account of St John's visit to Jane's cottage when he gives her a book of verse. You would need to be quite clear that this is the visit paid on 5 November, the evening of the holiday, and neither the first visit paid after her first day of teaching nor the third visit paid on 6 November when he tells her about the legacy and their relationship. If you give an account of the wrong visit you would score few, if any, marks.

(2) Make sure that you concentrate on the required part and on nothing else. Resist the temptation to relate what happens before or after. This would almost certainly be a waste of time and effort. Suppose you undertake the question:

Give an account of Jane's first meeting with Rochester

You could hardly fail to identify the correct part of the story, but you could still make the mistake of offering something like the following:

Paragraph 1: After Jane has been more than eight years at Lowood she begins to feel that she must move somewhere else . . . (another two or three sentences describing how she gets the Thornfield job).

Paragraph 2: So, late in October, she sets off for Millcote by coach . . . (another two sentences describing her journey to Thornfield).

Paragraph 3: She is kindly welcomed by . . . (another several sentences describing her arrival at Thornfield and starting work there).

Paragraph 4: One day in January Adèle has a cold . . . (some account of how this gives Jane a reason for walking to Hay).

Paragraph 5: On the way into Hay while Jane is sitting on a stile beside the frozen causeway . . . (leading into a description — all too brief — of her meeting with the horseman).

Paragraph 6: On her return to Thornfield Jane sees the dog . . . (further account of her discovery that the man she has met is, in fact, her employer, Mr Rochester).

The trouble with an essay along the lines given above is that it is too *dilute*. Everything it includes may be correct and well expressed, but the greater part of it has not been asked for and will not receive any marks. The fifth paragraph will be the only one actually to earn marks, and, however well written, it cannot be more than a very short answer indeed by itself. The following passage gives an example of a more suitable answer:

While walking into Hay on a cold winter afternoon Jane pauses to sit on a stile beside the long last hill into the village. It is near sunset and freezing cold, but the air is quiet and very still. She can see Thornfield in the valley below while the full moon rises above the horizon of the hill to the east. With her cloak gathered about her and her hands sheltering in her muff she is conscious of a strange hush, so absolute that she can actually hear the noises of life in Hay still far away.

This wintry peace is interrupted by the metallic clatter of an approaching horseman. Jane's desire to move is checked because the lane is so narrow that it seems sensible to stay on the stile until the rider has passed. Her mind is filled with romantic visions and fancies. She could almost believe it to be a ghost or apparition approaching her. Before the rider actually appears Jane sees a large dog, apparently his companion. Then comes the rider himself on a tall horse. Now the ghostly spell is broken and Jane is back in reality. Just after passing Jane the horse slips on the ice of the causeway. Horse and rider both fall. The man swears, the horse groans, and the dog barks. There is no one else there, and the dog seems to invite Jane's aid. So she goes up to the fallen rider and asks if she can do anything. While she is still standing there both horse and rider manage to scramble to their feet, but the man seems to be hurt and hobbles painfully to the stile where he can sit down.

Jane says that if he is hurt she will go to get help, but he answers that his injury is no more than a sprain, a twist of the ankle, not a broken bone. Jane observes him in the increasing moonlight. He seems to be a strong, dark, unattractive and not very agreeable man, between thirty and forty. Although he speaks roughly to her she is determined not to be put off by his manner. She repeats her desire to help. While he is still sitting on the stile he asks her who and what she is. A brief conversation tells him that she is governess at Thornfield.

Having learnt this much he asks her to try to catch his horse for him. She does her best but the animal is too restive and jerks away from her. It is obvious that she cannot do this. The man says he will have to catch the horse himself. As this means walking on his painful ankle he has to ask Jane to support him. He leans heavily on her shoulder and gets a hold on the horse's bridle. Once he has done this the rest is fairly easy. He leaps into the saddle, advises Jane to complete her mission into Hay quickly so that she can return to her home, and when she has handed him his whip which had fallen to the ground he rides off without delay.

Jane is left alone in the moonlit lane. Her first meeting with Mr Rochester is over.

Notice how this concentrated answer includes nothing outside the scope of the question.

---

(2) Recapitulation of selected parts

You may be asked to describe the part played by a particular character or element in the story. This requires you to retell or describe parts of the book that fulfil a given condition, and is a more demanding type of question. Selection becomes important. You must have a thorough knowledge of the book and yet be able to hold it at arm's length, so to speak, in order to select the suitable, reject the unsuitable material. It is necessary to understand precisely what you have to select, and to concentrate upon that selection. Suppose you are asked:

To what extent is Jane's life at Thornfield in contact with the existence of Bertha Rochester?

By careful selection and presentation of relevant material you should be able to produce an essay resembling the following model:

Jane actually sees Bertha Rochester twice only, two nights before and a few minutes after the broken wedding ceremony. But before ever seeing her she is made aware of her physical nearness several times.

During Jane's first day at Thornfield, after Mrs Fairfax has taken her out on the roof and as they return, Jane hears mysterious and sinister laughter coming from behind one of the locked doors at the top of the house. She is told it comes from Grace Poole, a resident servant, whom she sees being rebuked by Mrs Fairfax for making too much noise. Thereafter, whenever Jane hears similar laughter, she assumes it comes from her. This happens quite often during her first few months at Thornfield.

On the night after Mr Rochester has told her about Céline Varens Jane wakes up out of a fitful sleep. She hears a strange murmuring noise that she cannot understand. A little later, as the clock strikes two, she is aware that someone is trying to open her door. She thinks it may be the dog, Pilot, and feels easier. Then her fear is renewed when she hears weird demoniac laughter at her keyhole, close to the head of the bed. She hastily bolts the door; then hears retreating footsteps. Intending to go straight to Mrs Fairfax Jane leaves the room. There is smoke in the gallery. She traces it to Mr Rochester's room. He is lying unconscious on a bed already in flames. Jane promptly puts out the fire. When Mr Rochester has come to his senses he leaves the room to seek an explanation. He then encourages Jane to suppose that Grace Poole has started the fire.

There are no further manifestations of Bertha Rochester for several weeks. On the night after the arrival of Mason the silence of the night is suddenly broken by a terrifying scream. Then all are roused by fearful cries for help. Rochester sends all the guests to bed and then asks Jane to help him. Mason is lying on a bed in the third storey, wounded. Through a gap in the tapestry come the sounds of a caged animal, supposedly Grace Poole.

She does actually see Bertha for the first time two nights before the planned wedding. During the night she wakes up and sees a figure emerging from her closet. It is completely strange to her, a large dark woman, with black hair, bloodshot eyes, and a savage face. As Jane watches she tries on the veil, removes it, tears it in two and tramples on it. She then comes to the bed and leans over Jane who faints in terror. When Rochester hears of this he again says that it must have been Grace Poole. The whole experience has been more of a nightmare than reality to Jane.

Then she actually sees Bertha Rochester for what she is when they are taken up to her room just after the interrupted wedding. Described as a 'clothed hyena' the fearsome madwoman attacks Rochester while Jane and the others watch the grisly spectacle. She is bound to a chair and Jane never meets her again.

(3) Dealing with a particular feature or quality

You may be asked to deal with a certain aspect, feature or quality that is involved in the book. This may require you to detect this feature or quality, to recognise its nature, and detach it for the purpose of your essay. You need to make sure that you recognise and select correctly and that you do not offer irrelevant material. Suppose you are asked:

One of Jane's chief virtues is determination. Enlarge upon this statement. Here you must survey the whole of Jane's story in order to decide how much determination is displayed as she passes through childhood and adolescence to maturity. The difficulty is to avoid being swamped by too much material. Here is an example of how this question might be answered:

Jane's determination is a quality of unusual strength. Such a quality cannot operate in the absence of reasonable intelligence. In Jane's case, even when she is a child, she has an extraordinary capacity for clear thinking. She cannot accept anything less than the absolute truth. She has a very keen sense of right and wrong. When she exercises her determination she is in fact pursuing her concept of the true and the good with passionate intensity. This is regularly apparent at almost every successive crisis in her life.

After the departure of Mr Brocklehurst from Gateshead Jane sits and gazes at Mrs Reed with such force that Mrs Reed looks up and dismisses her. Jane starts to obey, but her feet will not carry her away from the room. She returns to confront Mrs Reed, summons up all her courage and embarks on a fierce denial of all the accusations made against her. Despite the obvious fact that Mrs Reed is accustomed to assert absolute control over the little child, Jane's passionate conviction actually wins this particular contest.

Jane's attitude to life at Lowood is coloured by the same determination. As soon as she is cleared of the accusation of being a liar by the arrival of a letter from Mr Lloyd, Jane's mind is sufficiently at rest for her to turn to the business of schooling. She sets about all the elements of the Lowood curriculum with typical industry and zeal. Here is something to be tackled, and her approach is as determined as one would expect of her. Of the rest of her time at Lowood we hear simply that Jane's life is not unhappy because she is not inactive. With a sound intelligence allied to her determination it is almost inevitable that she should rise to the head of the school, acquiring a very good education in the process.

In the face of a physical crisis or danger her resolution is no less strong. Inexperienced as she is, a horse thrashing about on a sheet of ice, a bedroom fire and a man bleeding from a stab wound in the middle of the night must all be alarmingly novel events. Jane faces them all with the calm self-reliance that one would expect in a person familiar with horses, fires and fighting. Her courage is largely the product of this attitude of determination.

But Jane's determination is most striking when she is confronted by a moral problem. After the interrupted marriage ceremony she is tested in the cruellest possible way. She is fully aware of her own love for Rochester, and makes no secret of it to him either. She submits to a long, passionate and persuasive argument that she should accept the compromise status of mistress because Bertha Rochester is so manifestly no wife in the true sense. And yet all the time that Rochester is pouring out his appeal there is no prospect that he will succeed. Jane knows what she must do. Before her conversation with him her mind gives the answer – 'Leave Thornfield at once', and this, she says, is prompt and dread. At the end of Rochester's persuasions the answer is still the same, although how hard it is, she says, to repeat firmly, 'I am going'. At no other time is her resolution so agonisingly tried, and she confesses in her narration that she could so easily yield to her master's love and accept his offer. Nevertheless, soon after midnight on that July night she gets up and leaves Thornfield. In the long hours of the summer morning she begins to despise herself for abandoning the master who loves and needs her, and yet, she says, it must be God that leads her on, for she is as determined as ever to reach the road and to leave the area. Thus she is herself astonished at the determination which is so strong, and almost, it seems, beyond her own control.

During the Morton period Jane's determination, if never quite so severely tested, is if anything stronger than ever with her increased maturity. Her attitude to the village school, to St John's arguments, to the splitting of the inheritance, and finally her response to the call for help, is invariably unshakeable. It is a very determined girl indeed who returns to Rochester in order to marry and look after him.

(4) Explanation

Questions in this category simply invite you to explain some aspect of the book.

You may choose a question in this category if you feel confident that you know the essence of the answer required, and that a statement of this answer will occupy neither more nor much less than the writing time available. The usual need for relevance applies. Suppose you are asked:

Why do you think that Charlotte Brontë makes Rochester almost totally blind for some time and then allows him to recover some of his sight?

This question may be adequately answered in rather less space than an examination essay would normally occupy. You can afford, therefore, to treat this subject in some detail. Here is a treatment:

> Throughout the story of Jane Eyre there are several indications that when Jane is finally in a position to 'give her heart' she will do this with her usual passionate intensity and generosity.
>
> On the evening of the gipsy impersonation, when Rochester is shocked by the information that Mason has arrived, Jane says to him 'Can I help you, sir? – I'd give my life to serve you'. And a few weeks later, on her return from Gateshead, she declares to Rochester, 'I have talked face to face with what I reverence, with what I delight in – I have known you, Mr Rochester, and it strikes me with terror and anguish to feel I must be absolutely torn from you for ever'.
>
> Many Victorians were shocked that Jane could make such passionate declarations to a man to whom she is not betrothed. She is certainly not the woman to hold anything back; she will give her all.
>
> When, a year later, Jane does marry the man she has loved for so long it is like the bursting of a dam. Her love pours out and she will do anything in 'her Edward's service'.
>
> Thus the fact that Rochester is so helpless when she marries him has enriched the early years of their marriage. Jane says she knows what it is to live entirely for and with the man she loves best on earth. They are ever together. They talk all day long. She supplies his lack of sight by reading to him and by observing the normal life around them.
>
> He, for his part, reciprocates her love so totally that he accepts her joyous service as fully as she gives it. His dependence on her makes their union deeper, their love more tender, their physical relationship more intimate.
>
> There can be little doubt that Charlotte Brontë intends the first phase of their marriage to be all the finer and more splendid for Rochester's weakness and Jane's strength. It is also the final demonstration that Jane is the greater spirit of the two.
>
> Her decision to restore some sight to Rochester's better eye seems perfectly permissible 'novelist's licence', although it is not clear whether it is medically probable. After two years of utter dependence upon Jane has created a bond of love between them that will last for ever it seems a harmless and pleasant conclusion to the romance that the rest of their married life should be eased in this way. He has been punished enough. We are glad that he is allowed to see his son.

(5) Comparison

You may be asked to compare one character with another, one relationship with another, or one state of affairs with another. Sometimes examiners use the term 'Compare and contrast . . .' Whether they do or not you are expected to state ways in which the two are alike and other ways in which they are unlike.

The best way of making a comparison is to set out a sort of tabulated ladder, and then apply several tests or factors in turn to the couple compared. Suppose you are asked:

Compare Rochester and St John Rivers in their dealings with people other than Jane

This is a restricted comparison. Jane is excluded. Do not refer to her. After Jane these two men are the most important characters in the work and they invite comparison. Here is a specimen answer:

We see a great deal of both these characters in varying situations and with people of different types and social ranks. Our assessment of their characters springs mainly from the conduct of their human relationships.

Rochester and St John are both men of authority. Rochester's authority derives mainly from his status as a landowner, a man of wealth and inherited power. St John's authority is due more to his profession as clergyman. His rank, socially, is not strictly inferior to Rochester's, for it is well established that the Rivers family is ancient and honourable, but the family is now much poorer in both land and fortune, and if he were not a clergyman St John would certainly not be in a position to behave as authoritatively as he does.

Both Rochester and St John tend to speak with confident authority to anyone they meet. But while Rochester's manner to inferiors is autocratic it is at least hearty, while St John's manner is bleak and distant even with the one servant, Hannah, whom the Rivers family can now afford.

For relatives St John has two sisters while Rochester has but a single ward (he does not treat Mrs Fairfax as a member of his family). St John's manner to Diana and Mary is cool and detached. Even if he is not actually rude to them he is neither considerate nor affectionate. Adèle, of course, is still a child and treated as such, without any ceremony, when Rochester needs to speak to her at all.

With persons of his own rank Rochester continues to behave in an entirely dominant way. He manages all his guests, including Lord and Lady Ingram, Colonel Dent, Sir George and Lady Lynn, with complete self-assurance, and they seem quite prepared to follow his lead. We never see St John in comparable company but we can observe him with the wealthy Mr Oliver. There is no question of St John's acceding meekly to Mr Oliver's wishes, and he rejects Rosamond's persuasion that he should call on her father at Vale Hall.

Both Rochester and St John are nearly always confident that they know best, that they must be in the right. Their confidence is shown in medical matters. Rochester is perfectly satisfied that he can assess Mason's condition better than the surgeon Carter. It is Carter who asks Rochester if Mason is fit to be moved, not the other way round. As for St John, he is equally confident that there is no need to send for a physician to examine the exhausted Jane. He pronounces his medical judgement on Jane as dogmatically as Rochester pronounced his on Mason.

There is thus a great deal of similarity between the two men. They are both as dominating as circumstances permit. It would hardly be an exaggeration to say that they are both unhesitating autocrats. Rochester is much the more genial of the two but they both ride roughshod over all who come in their way – except, of course, for Jane.

(6) Opinion and criticism

Your opinion may be invited in all sorts of ways. You may simply be asked to express it directly, or you may be given someone else's opinion and asked how much you agree with it. Such questions nearly always end with the instruction, 'Discuss' or 'Comment', with the question, 'Do you agree?' or 'How true is this?'

These questions are seldom easy, but if you think that you have a good opportunity to express your strong or warmly felt approval, and are confident that you have powerful arguments to support it, you may decide that this would be a good line to follow.

Sincerity and enthusiasm are important, and can provide a valuable starting point. Suppose you are asked:

'Although Jane and Rochester seem very different they actually have a great deal in common.' Discuss.

In this case you might start with a statement of exactly why they seem very different – easy enough – and then advance to the main part of your answer, which would be a formulation of the great deal they are alleged to have in common. This is more difficult but might lead to an essay like the following:

We are familiar with Jane, through her own narrative, long before Rochester enters the story. As soon as he begins to exist as a new and increasingly significant figure we are aware of qualities that are wholly new and almost entirely different.

To begin with the differences are so striking as to make any possibility of similarities inconceivable. Jane is young, poor and simple. Rochester is approaching middle-age, rich and sophisticated. She has seen nothing of the outside world, whereas he has travelled to the West Indies, St Petersburg, and the cities of Italy. He occupies a position of inherited wealth and power; she has no place in the world that she does not achieve by her own efforts. When the house party assembles Jane is aware of being despised while he is generally admired.

Gradually, however, we begin to see there are items in the balance sheet working the other way. She is morally innocent; his life has been sinful. She is totally honest; he can be evasive and deceitful. For her the truth overrides everything; for him the truth, if unwelcome, may be something he will try to evade.

Even their early conversations quickly become the communion of intelligent and active brains. In conversation alone Jane is never inferior. She may say less, she may speak more cautiously – not always – but she can always hold her own with him in sense and self-expression.

They share a freedom from petty jealousy. When Rochester tells Jane of his betrayal by his Parisian mistress he confesses that his first reaction is one of savage jealousy. He then discovers that the man concerned is a feeble fellow (though a Vicomte) and all jealousy evaporates. The man does not deserve it. Jane's feeling towards Blanche is oddly similar. She concedes the outward charms and social gifts, and then goes on to relate that Miss Ingram is beneath jealousy, because she is too inferior. This is astonishing. Is Jane being guilty of a sudden outburst of vanity, or is malice making her stupid? Not at all. Jane is simply conscious of something in herself that is bigger than anything in Blanche Ingram, just as Rochester has felt contempt for the French Vicomte.

In several profound ways Rochester and Jane are well matched. They are both keenly intelligent, far superior to any other characters in the book, except perhaps to Miss Temple and Helen Burns who have disappeared. In their sense of human values and self-knowledge they are again well-matched. They both have great strength of character, a quality that is not easy to define. Perhaps the word *magnanimity*, or sheer bigness of spirit, like Bunyan's *Mr Greatheart*, comes near to explaining it.

The one quality in which they are unequal is that of moral strength and spiritual honesty. In these respects it is Jane who is the stronger.

It is thus appropriate that the book should end, not simply with the union of two noble spirits, but also with the weaker finding refuge and protection with the strong.

The language of the examination answer

Try to express your answers in simple and straightforward English. Do not allow yourself to be affected by Charlotte Brontë's style, and do not imitate her. Your task is to say what you think needs to be said clearly and economically.

It is probably sensible always to use the present sequence of narration. Avoid shifting from one sequence to another or, even more dangerous, using both in a single sentence.

Nearly all examination answers are written under some time pressure. You may need to pack a lot of information into a small space. Do not be afraid to use a blunt, compact style. Short sentences may be a sign of strength, not weakness.

It is most unlikely that you will ever need to quote from the text. Avoid memorising fragments, and be prepared to write about the book in your own words.

During the final stages of preparing for an examination do not think that revision must consist solely of reading and re-reading. Wise revision also includes some *writing* – to keep your hand in – some *talking* about the book with your friends, and some *thinking* about it as well. The amount of knowledge you take into the examination matters less than having that knowledge well arranged and available for whatever essays you choose to write.

Part 5

Suggestions for further reading

The text

Jane Eyre, Penguin English Library, Penguin Books, Harmondsworth, 1966. This edition has a valuable introduction by Q. D. Leavis and extensive notes on points of particular interest. The novel is also available in Everyman's Library, Dent, London. This edition has a useful introduction by Margaret Lane, a select bibliography, but no notes.

General reading

GASKELL, ELIZABETH: *The Life of Charlotte Brontë*, edited by Alan Shelston. Penguin English Library, Penguin Books, Harmondsworth, 1975. This is also available in an Everyman's Library Edition, Dent, London, 1971.

BENSON, E. F.: *Charlotte Brontë*, Longman, London, 1933.

CECIL, LORD DAVID: *Early Victorian Novelists,* Constable, London, 1963.

BENTLEY, PHYLLIS: *The Brontës,* 2nd ed, Arthur Barker, London, 1966.

LANE, MARGARET: *The Brontë Story*, Heinemann, London, 1966.

GERIN, WINIFRED: *Charlotte Brontë, the evolution of genius,* Oxford University Press, Oxford, 1967.

BENTLEY, PHYLLIS: *The Brontës and their World*, Thames and Hudson, London, 1969.

MORRISON, NANCY BRYSSON: *Haworth Harvest*, Dent, London, 1969.

BENTLEY, PHYLLIS: *The Brontë Sisters* in the Writers and their Work series, Longman, Harlow, for the British Council.

The author of these notes

BARTY KNIGHT was educated at St John's College, Cambridge, and has spent many years in Ethiopia, East Africa and the Middle East, mainly in schools or colleges of education. He was Principal of Dar es Salaam College of Education for five years and of Brummana High School, Lebanon, for seven years. He has written on various educational topics and on producing open-air Shakespeare.